Putting Out the Fire

SMOKING AND THE LAW

Tobacco: The Deadly Drug

Putting Out the Fire

SMOKING AND THE LAW

by
Joyce Libal

Putting Out the Fire: Smoking and the Law

MASON CREST PUBLISHERS INC.
370 Reed Road
Broomall, Pennsylvania 19008
(866)MCP-BOOK (toll free)
www.masoncrest.com

First Printing

9 8 7 6 5 4 3 2 1

ISBN 978-1-4222-0234-0
ISBN 978-1-4222-0230-2 (series)
        Library of Congress Cataloging-in-Publication Data

Libal, Joyce.
Putting out the fire : smoking and the law / Joyce Libal.
        p. cm. — (Tobacco: the deadly drug)
  Includes bibliographical references and index.
  ISBN 978-1-4222-0234-0   ISBN 978-1-4222-1331-5
  1. Smoking—Law and legislation—United States. 2. Tobacco—Law and legislation—United States. I. Title.
  KF3812.3.L53 2009
  344.7305′4—dc22
                                        2008019477

Design by MK Bassett-Harvey.
Produced by Harding House Publishing Service, Inc.
www.hardinghousepages.com
Cover design by Peter Culotta.
Printed in The United States of America.

Contents

Introduction

Tobacco has been around for centuries. In fact, it played a major role in the early history of the United States. Tobacco use has fallen into and out of popularity, sometimes based on gender roles or class, or more recently, because of its effects on health. The books in the Mason Crest series TOBACCO: THE DEADLY DRUG, provide readers with a look at many aspects of tobacco use. Most important, the series takes a serious look at why smoking is such a hard habit to break, even with all of the available information about its harmful effects.

The primary ingredient in tobacco products that keeps people coming back for another cigarette is nicotine. Nicotine is a naturally occurring chemical in the tobacco plant. As plants evolved over millions of years, they developed the ability to produce chemical defenses against being eaten by animals. Nicotine is the tobacco plant's chemical defense weapon. Just as too much nicotine can make a person feel dizzy and nauseated, so the same thing happens to animals that might otherwise eat unlimited quantities of the tobacco plant.

Nicotine, in small doses, produces mildly pleasurable (rewarding) experiences, leading many people to dose themselves repeatedly throughout the day. People carefully dose themselves with nicotine to maximize the rewarding experience. These periodic hits of tobacco also help people avoid unpleasant (toxic) effects, such as dizziness, nausea, trembling, and sweating, which can occur when someone takes in an excessive amount of nicotine. These unpleasant effects are sometimes seen when a person smokes for the first time.

Although nicotine is the rewarding component of cigarettes, it is not the cause of many diseases that trouble smokers, such as lung cancer, heart attacks, and strokes. Many of the thousands of other chemicals in the ciga-

rette are responsible for the increased risk for these diseases among smokers. In some cases, medical research
has identified cancer-causing chemicals in the burning
cigarette. More research is needed, because our understanding of exactly how cigarette smoking causes many
forms of cancer, lung diseases (emphysema, bronchitis),
heart attacks, and strokes is limited, as is our knowledge
on the effects of secondhand smoke.

The problem with smoking also involves addiction.
But what is addiction? Addiction refers to a pattern of
behavior, lasting months to years, in which a person
engages in the intense, daily use of a pleasure-producing
(rewarding) activity, such as smoking. This type of use
has medically and personally negative effects for the person. As an example of negative medical consequences,
consider that heavy smoking (nicotine addiction) leads
to heart attacks and lung cancer. As an example of negative personal consequences, consider that heavy smoking may cause a loss of friendship, because the friend
can't tolerate the smoke and/or the odor.

Nicotine addiction includes tolerance and withdrawal. New smokers typically start with fewer than
five cigarettes per day. Gradually, as the body becomes
adapted to the presence of nicotine, greater amounts
are required to obtain the same rewarding effects, and
the person eventually smokes fifteen to twenty or more
cigarettes per day. This is tolerance, meaning that more
drug is needed to achieve the same rewarding effects.
The brain becomes "wired" differently after long-term
exposure to nicotine, allowing the brain to tolerate levels of nicotine that would otherwise be toxic and cause
nausea, vomiting, dizziness and anxiety.

When a heavy smoker abruptly stops smoking, irritability, headache, sleeplessness, anxiety, and difficulty
concentrating all develop within half a day and trouble

the smoker for one to two weeks. These withdrawal effects are generally the opposite of those produced by the drug. They are another external sign that the brain has become wired differently because of long-term exposure to nicotine. The withdrawal effects described above are accompanied by craving. For the nicotine addict, craving is a state of mind in which having a cigarette seems the most important thing in life at the moment. For the nicotine addict, craving is a powerful urge to smoke.

Nicotine addiction, then, can be understood as heavy, daily use over months to years (with tolerance and withdrawal), despite negative consequences. Now that we have definitions of *nicotine* and *addiction*, why read the books in this series? The answer is simple: tobacco is available everywhere to persons of all ages. The books in the series TOBACCO: THE DEADLY DRUG are about understanding the beginnings, natural history, and consequences of nicotine addiction. If a teenager smokes at least one cigarette daily for a month, that person has an 80 percent chance of becoming a lifetime, nicotine-addicted, daily smoker, with all the negative consequences.

But the series is not limited to those topics. What are the characteristic beginnings of nicotine addiction? Nicotine addiction typically begins between the ages of twelve and twenty, when most young people decide to try a first cigarette. Because cigarettes are available everywhere in our society, with little restriction on purchase, nearly everyone is faced with the decision to take a puff from that first cigarette. Whether this first puff leads to a lifetime of nicotine addiction depends on several factors. Perhaps the most important factor is DNA (genetics), as twin studies tell us that most of the risk for nicotine addiction is genetic, but there is a large role for nongenetic factors (environment), such as the smoking habits of friends. Research is needed to identify the specific genetic and environmental factors that shape a person's decision to continue to smoke after that first cigarette. Books in the series also address how peer pressure and biology affect one's likelihood of smoking and possibly becoming addicted.

It is difficult to underestimate the power of nicotine addiction. It causes smokers to continue to smoke despite life-threatening events. When heavy smokers have a heart attack, a life-threatening event often directly related to smoking, they spend a week or more in the hospital where they cannot smoke. So they are discharged after enforced abstinence. Even though they realize that smoking contributed strongly to the heart attack, half of them return to their former smoking habits within three weeks of leaving the hospital. This decision to return to smoking increases the risk of a second heart attack. Nicotine addiction can influence powerfully the choices we make, often prompting us to make choices that put us at risk.

TOBACCO: THE DEADLY DRUG doesn't stop with the whys and the hows of smoking and addiction. The series includes books that provide readers with tools they can use to not take that first cigarette, how they can stand up to negative peer pressure, and know when they are being unfairly influenced by the media. And if they do become smokers, books in the series provide information about how they can stop.

If nicotine addiction can be a powerful negative effect, then giving people information that might help them decide to avoid—or stop—smoking makes sense. That is what TOBACCO: THE DEADLY DRUG is all about.

— *Wade Berrettini MD, PhD*

CHAPTER 1

Glossary

carcinogens: substances that cause cancer.

clandestine: secret, not meant for general knowledge.

consensus: agreement among all members of a group.

surgeon general: the cabinet-level public health officer of the United States.

tolerance: the reduction in the normal response to a substance due to prolonged use or exposure.

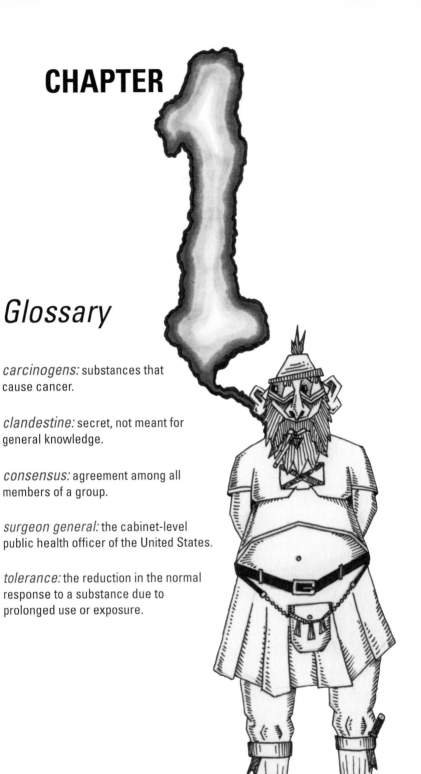

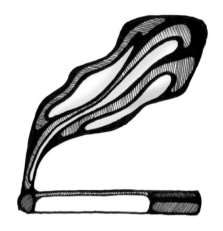

A Brief Look at Tobacco and Health

Tobacco has been an important part of American history for centuries. People in South America began using tobacco thousands of years ago, and as Native Americans traveled into Central and North America, they brought the powerful plant with them. Likewise, the first European explorers and conquerors to visit the Western Hemisphere began to use tobacco, and the habit soon spread across the globe.

As the United States expanded westward during the late eighteenth century and early nineteenth century, so did the use of tobacco. In those days, all people knew about tobacco was how they felt when they were smoking or chewing it, or

In the early part of the twentieth century, the use of tobacco led to a huge increase in the number of people who suffered from respiratory diseases like lung cancer and emphysema

what they observed in others who were using the plant. Before the twentieth century, nothing was known about the long-term health effects of tobacco.

No one saw any reason to stop tobacco use. After all, it made people feel good. During the First World War, the government even provided cigarettes to soldiers because they helped the men endure boredom and calmed their nerves before battles. Cigarette smoking was seen as a harmless social activity.

A Growing Health Crisis

Like many things that at first seem innocent enough, doubts eventually grew about the harmlessness of cigarette smoking. People noticed their growing dependence on it. What started for many as recreation soon became an absolute necessity, without which they were both mentally and physically uncomfortable. As smokers built up a *tolerance* to tobacco, they needed to increase the number of cigarettes they smoked each day to achieve the same feelings.

> **FAST FACT**
> The Vaccine Act of 1813 was the first federal law dealing with consumer protection and therapeutic substances.
> (*Source*: FDA Web Site, www.fda.gov)

After decades of cigarette use, some Americans began to believe that a health crisis was emerging. Before 1900, hardly anyone in the United States died from lung cancer. By the mid-1930s, lung cancer claimed approximately 4,000 lives annually. The growing number of lung cancer cases was not the only problem, either. Other types of cancer, as well as emphysema and heart disease, were also on the increase.

Cigarettes Cause Disease

By the 1950s, scientific researchers were discovering a link between smoking and disease. "Cancer by the Carton," an essay published in *Reader's Digest* in 1952, was one of the first articles to inform the public of these dangers.

In 1960, Helmut Wakeham, head of research and development for Philip Morris, found that cigarette smoke contained forty-two *carcinogens*. (Today we know that tobacco smoke contains thousands of dangerous chemicals.) In 1961, an article appeared in the *New England Journal of Medicine* stating that, "Most of the evidence . . . demonstrates a close association between heavy cigarette smoking and lung cancer."

In 1962, the Royal College of Physicians (RCP) in England issued its first major report on smoking. It said:

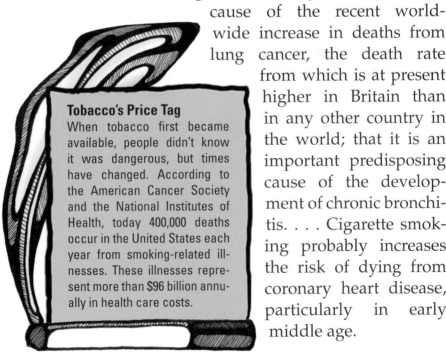

> Cigarette smoking is a cause of lung cancer and bronchitis. . . . Cigarette smoking is the most likely cause of the recent worldwide increase in deaths from lung cancer, the death rate from which is at present higher in Britain than in any other country in the world; that it is an important predisposing cause of the development of chronic bronchitis. . . . Cigarette smoking probably increases the risk of dying from coronary heart disease, particularly in early middle age.

Tobacco's Price Tag
When tobacco first became available, people didn't know it was dangerous, but times have changed. According to the American Cancer Society and the National Institutes of Health, today 400,000 deaths occur in the United States each year from smoking-related illnesses. These illnesses represent more than $96 billion annually in health care costs.

After the release of the report by the RCP, the U.S. *surgeon general*, Dr. Luther Leonidas Terry, appointed an advisory committee to report on the issue in the United States. By 1964, most scientists had reached a *consensus*. Their findings were represented in *Smoking and Health: Report of the Advisory Committee to the Surgeon General of the United States*, which concluded that there was a link between cigarette smoking and lung cancer and bronchitis. It also said there was reason to believe that smoking played a role in causing other types of cancer, cardiovascular disease, and emphysema.

In 1979, the surgeon general's report issued by Dr. Julius B. Richmond said smoking:

is a significant causative factor in the cancer of the larynx . . . is a significant causal factor in the

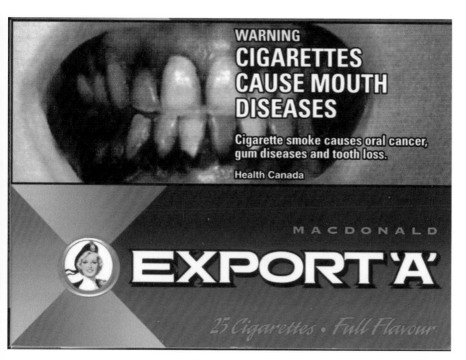

Today, no one doubts the fact that cigarettes can cause many harmful diseases. In fact, governments ensure that people know this by requiring warnings on the labels on all tobacco products.

development of oral cancer . . . is a causal factor in the development of cancer of the esophagus . . . is related to the cancer of the pancreas . . . is one of the three major independent risk factors for heart attack.

FAST FACT
Until 1972, the U.S. government provided cigarettes as part of a soldier's daily meal ration.

In 1982, Surgeon General C. Everett Koop confirmed the previous reports issued by past surgeons general about tobacco use and concluded that smoking was, "the chief, single, avoidable cause of death in our society, and the most important public health issue of our time." Between 1964 and 2006, the surgeon general's office issued twenty-nine reports on smoking and health.

The Addictive Quality of Nicotine

During the early 1950s, as the health consequences of smoking were starting to be studied, scientists also began to recognize that nicotine, the principal active chemical in tobacco, was highly addictive. This explained why people who smoked or chewed tobacco could not easily stop using the stuff. Many people in the tobacco industry recognized the addictive quality of nicotine, and what that meant for sales of their products. In one British American Tobacco Company document written during the 1950s, the author commented that the company should not try to reduce the amount of nicotine in its cigarettes. The memo noted, "To lower nicotine too much might end up destroying the nicotine habit in a large number of consumers and prevent it from ever being acquired by new smokers."

Cigarette manufacturers were studying the effects of this tobacco component in a *clandestine* way. In 1962, the Board of Directors of British American Tobacco received a memo from Sir Charles Ellis, the company's scientific director. It read, "As a result of these various researches, we now possess a knowledge of the effects of nicotine far more extensive than exists in published scientific literature." Internal documents revealed in later court cases showed that by 1971, the Philip Morris tobacco company understood that nicotine withdrawal effects were associated with quitting smoking, making it difficult if not almost impossible for some people to stop smoking.

By the 1960s, scientests were beginning to figure out the correlation between smoking and health problems. They reported their findings to the Surgeon General in a report made in 1964.

By 1988, when Surgeon General Dr. C. Everett Koop, issued a report stating that the nicotine in cigarettes was addictive, nearly every organization involved in public health recognized nicotine as the cause of addiction to cigarettes.

Over the years, however, industry representatives denied and belittled these scientific findings in public. In a television interview, James Morgan, the president and CEO of Philip Morris, compared an addiction to cigarettes to his own professed "addiction" to gummi bears. On another occasion, Dr. Christopher Coggins, the senior vice president of science and technology at Lorillard, said smoking was no more addictive than "sugar and salt and Internet access." In 2004, Susan Ivey, who had been a CEO at both Brown & Williamson Tobacco Co. and R. J. Reynolds, said, "The company would not agree that nicotine is an addictive drug." And as late as 2005, a representative of Lorillard admitted that smoking is addictive, but said tobacco's addictive quality is the same as other "repetitive pleasurable activities that can be difficult to stop." The representative went on to say that smoking is not addictive in a "pharmacological sense."

Shadow of a Doubt

After the release of the 1964 surgeon general's report, the public became more worried about smoking. Concern among government policy makers also grew. How did the tobacco industry react? Cigarette companies wanted to keep sales at maximum levels, and they did not want new laws regulating their products.

To achieve these goals, they spent decades casting doubt on the scientific community's research linking

C. Everett Koop, United States Surgeon General (1982-1989).

smoking to disease. Industry representatives in both the United States and England continued to claim that tobacco had not been "proven" to cause cancer and denied that there was a consensus among scientists.

After the RCP issued its report in 1962, John Partridge, an executive for the Imperial Tobacco Company, appeared on a BBC television program. He said he did not accept the "sweeping assertions" of the RCP report and that it presented an "unbalanced picture." He continued, "I do not believe that you will stop the people of this country from smoking. . . . They know the odds are heavily against their coming to any real harm from it." When asked about advertising, he went on to say that Imperial would continue advertising to young people, though not to children.

Tobacco Withdrawal Symptoms
These are a few of the withdrawal symptoms smokers may experience when they quit abruptly. Fortunately, most go away after a few weeks.

- anxiety
- cigarette cravings
- constipation
- decreased heart rate
- depression
- difficulty concentrating
- fatigue
- headache
- increased appetite
- increased coughing
- insomnia
- irritability or anger
- restlessness
- tremors

In a 1982 U.S. television interview, R. J. Reynolds' chairman of the board said, "It is not known whether cigarettes cause cancer." And in a 1990 letter written to an elementary school student and the school's principal, a public relations specialist for R. J. Reynolds wrote, "Despite all the research going on, the simple and unfortunate fact is that scientists do not know the cause or causes of the chronic diseases reported to be associated with smoking."

Despite their public denials of the increasing amount of scientific research that was coming to the fore about smoking's dangers, something was going on behind closed doors at the tobacco industry. Like most secrets, theirs would eventually be revealed.

CHAPTER 2

Glossary

august: marked by dignity and serious purpose.

mortality: death or death rate.

plaintiffs: people who bring a legal action.

Big Bad Tobacco: Secrets Revealed

For decades, the dangers of tobacco use were not well understood, at least not by many scientists working for the government. But what did the cigarette industry know about the dangers of tobacco, and when did Big Tobacco know it?

The Paper Trail

Despite what tobacco companies were saying publicly, evidence eventually came to light about when they realized that nicotine was addictive and when they knew that smoking caused disease. That evidence lies in a paper trail hidden for years within the industry. Many of these internal company memorandums have now been unearthed for all to see.

The Mouse House
This was the nickname of an R. J. Reynolds research facility established in the 1960s that used mice and rabbits to study the health effects of smoking. Research conducted there showed a link between smoking and emphysema. In 1970, R. J. Reynolds closed the facility, destroyed the research papers, fired the twenty-six scientists employed there, and prohibited them from publishing their findings or discussing them publicly.

In 1953, Claude Teague of R. J. Reynolds wrote in an internal memo, "Studies of clinical data tend to confirm the relationship between heavy and prolonged tobacco smoking and incidence of cancer of the lung." A memo written at the Brown & Williamson Tobacco Company in 1978 described nicotine as addictive and even a poison.

But tobacco companies also understood the importance of nicotine in cigarettes. William Dunn, a scientist working for Philip Morris, wrote a memo explaining that without nicotine, "The cigarette market would collapse, P.M. [Philip Morris] would collapse, and we'd all lose our jobs and consulting fees."

Despite the frank nature of this internal correspondence, industry representatives continued to belittle the scientific evidence and deliberately misrepresent the scientific findings about tobacco in public. Representatives of tobacco companies denied that smoking caused cancer when they testified before the U.S. House of Representatives Subcommittee on Health and the Environment in 1994. Continuous denial of scientific evidence was part of an orchestrated strategy. In a court ruling in 2006, the judge found that tobacco companies had known smoking caused disease for at least fifty or sixty

Even the tobacco companies themselves realized how dangerous nicotine could be in the development of tobacco addiction. However, they denied these findings when testifiying before the U.S. House of Representatives in 1994.

years and that internal company documents indicated that they conducted a calculated campaign to "deny and distort" scientific evidence.

Smokescreens and Dodgy Science

A 1964 memorandum from George Weissman, executive vice president overseas (international) for Philip Morris, to Joseph F. Cullman, also of Philip Morris, said, "We must in the near future provide some answers which will give smokers a psychological crutch and a self-rationale to continue smoking." According to Judge Gladys Kessler, who presided over *United States of America v. Philip Morris USA Inc.*, et al., that memo was written in response to the 1964 surgeon general's report. Weissman went on to suggest that one of the "crutches" or "rationales" his company could use to counter medical evidence was that "more research is needed." He further suggested that tobacco company representatives note that there were "discrepancies" and "contradictions" in the report.

Many people now believe the tobacco industry was also trying to fool the public by setting up organizations in the early 1960s with prestigious, scientific-sounding names. These included the Tobacco Institute, which handled much of the industry's public relations, and the Tobacco Industry's Research Committee (TIRC), later called the Council for Tobacco Research (CTR). The primary purpose

Smoking Beagles

In 1970, the *New York Times* published an article on a scientific study, conducted under the auspices of the American Cancer Society, that exposed dogs to cigarette smoke. This was the first study to prove that lung cancer developed in large animals that smoked.

Many of the chemical components of cigarette smoke are highly toxic.

The chemicals in tobacco smoke can narrow the veins in the heart, leading to an increased chance of heart attack.

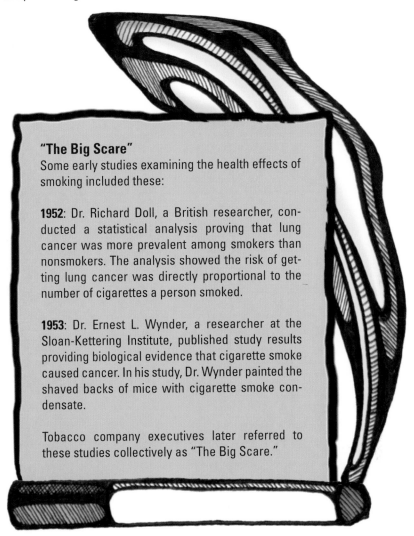

"The Big Scare"
Some early studies examining the health effects of smoking included these:

1952: Dr. Richard Doll, a British researcher, conducted a statistical analysis proving that lung cancer was more prevalent among smokers than nonsmokers. The analysis showed the risk of getting lung cancer was directly proportional to the number of cigarettes a person smoked.

1953: Dr. Ernest L. Wynder, a researcher at the Sloan-Kettering Institute, published study results providing biological evidence that cigarette smoke caused cancer. In his study, Dr. Wynder painted the shaved backs of mice with cigarette smoke condensate.

Tobacco company executives later referred to these studies collectively as "The Big Scare."

of these organizations was to help the tobacco industry continue denying smoking's alleged role in causing illnesses such as cancer and heart disease. The Scientific Advisory Board of TIRC, for example, issued a report in 1960 titled *Causation Theory of Smoking Unproved*. It came to the conclusion that "the causation theory of smoking in lung cancer, heart disease and other ailments is without clinical and experimental proof." In 1962, the TIRC said the report by the UK's Royal College of Physicians contained "no new or original data but amounts to a statement of opinion." It called the report "a disservice to scientific research." In 1988, Judge H. Lee Sarokin of the U.S. District Court in Newark, New Jersey, presiding over *Cipollone v. Liggett Group, Philip Morris, and Loews*, said it would be easy to conclude that the TIRC was "nothing but a hoax created for public relations purposes with no intention of seeking the truth or publishing it."

And what of the Tobacco Institute? A press release issued by this *august*-sounding body in 1962 stated:

> The causes of cancer are not now known to science. Many factors are being studied along with tobacco. The case against tobacco is based largely on statistical association, the meanings of which are in dispute.

The Tobacco Institute called the surgeon general's 1964 report a "shockingly intemperate defamation of an industry which has led the way in medical research to seek answers in the cigarette controversy." And in 1978, it published a pamphlet stating, "The flat assertion that smoking causes lung cancer and heart disease and that the case is proved is not supported by many of the world's leading scientists."

Tobacco-Funded Scientific Research

In 1963, The Liggett Group, Inc., hired Arthur D. Little, a consulting firm, to write a report the company intended to submit to the surgeon general. When the report concluded that there was "a causal relationship between

"A Frank Statement to Cigarette Smokers"

In response to publicity generated by unbiased scientific studies, several tobacco companies published a full-page newspaper ad in 1954 titled "A Frank Statement to Cigarette Smokers." The ad ran in 448 American newspapers and reached more than 43 million readers. These are some of the claims made in the "Frank Statement":

- Recent reports on experiments with mice have given wide publicity to a theory that cigarette smoking is in some way linked with lung cancer.
- Although conducted by doctors of professional standing, these experiments are not regarded as conclusive in the field of cancer research.
- There is no proof that cigarette smoking is one of the causes [of lung cancer].
- We accept an interest in people's health as a basic responsibility.
- We believe the products we make are not injurious to health.
- We always have and always will cooperate closely with those whose task it is to safeguard the public health.
- We are pledging aid and assistance for research into all phases of tobacco use and health.
- For this purpose we are establishing a joint industry group consisting initially of the undersigned. This group will be known as [the] Tobacco Industry Research Committee.
- In charge of the research activities of the Committee will be a scientist of unimpeachable integrity and national repute. In addition there will be an Advisory Board of scientists disinterested in the cigarette industry. A group of distinguished men from medicine, science, and education will be invited to serve on this Board. These scientists will advise the Committee on its research activities.
- This statement is being issued because we believe the people are entitled to know where we stand on this matter and what we intend to do about it.

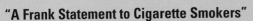

chemical properties of ingested tobacco smoke and the development of carcinoma" and that smoking cigarettes caused increased *mortality* "for coronary artery diseases, for all carcinoma combined, for lung cancer, for genitor-urinary system cancers and for cancers of the buccal cavity [throat and mouth]," Liggett decided not to submit it.

An earlier draft of the "Frank Statement" shows tobacco companies considered and then deleted the following text: "We will never produce and market a product shown to be the cause of any serious human ailment.... The Committee will undertake to keep the public informed of such facts as may be developed relating to cigarette smoking and health and other pertinent matters."

Over the years, the tobacco industry has spent millions financing scientific research, but most of it has been aimed at proving that cigarettes are harmless. But when studies began to show that cigarettes were indeed harmful, tobacco companies often stopped financing the research. At Harvard in 1980, for example, Dr. Gary Huber was using animal studies to conduct tobacco-funded research on a possible link between smoking and health issues. Eventually, the industry cut off Dr. Huber's funding. Lawyers for Big Tobacco told Dr. Huber he was "getting too close to some things."

Cigarette Advertising

While the health controversy raged, tobacco companies continued to spend millions on cigarette advertisements. Some advertising dollars were directly aimed at confusing the health issue in the minds of the public. R.

J. Reynolds lavished millions of dollars on a campaign that told Americans:

> Can we have an open debate about smoking? Over the years you've heard so many negative reports about smoking and health—and so little to challenge these reports—that you may assume the case against smoking is closed. But this is far from the truth. Studies which conclude that smoking causes disease have regularly ignored significant evidence to the contrary.

Ironically, at the same time that cigarette companies were telling the public that cigarettes were safe, they began marketing so-called *low-tar* and *light* cigarettes they declared were "safer." This effort to reassure smokers by offering them healthier cigarettes was another method used to persuade smokers not to quit. Scientific evidence has shown that these cigarettes are just as harmful as regular ones.

Over the years, the secret paper trail and public advertising by tobacco companies have combined to form a mountain of evidence that *plaintiffs* in both federal and state lawsuits have used against the industry.

Because tobacco has been available in the United States since the country's earliest days, it came on the scene without regulation. It took decades for science and the government to prove that cigarette smoking posed a danger to human health. As understanding of the product's harmful effects increased, however, the government passed many laws to regulate tobacco.

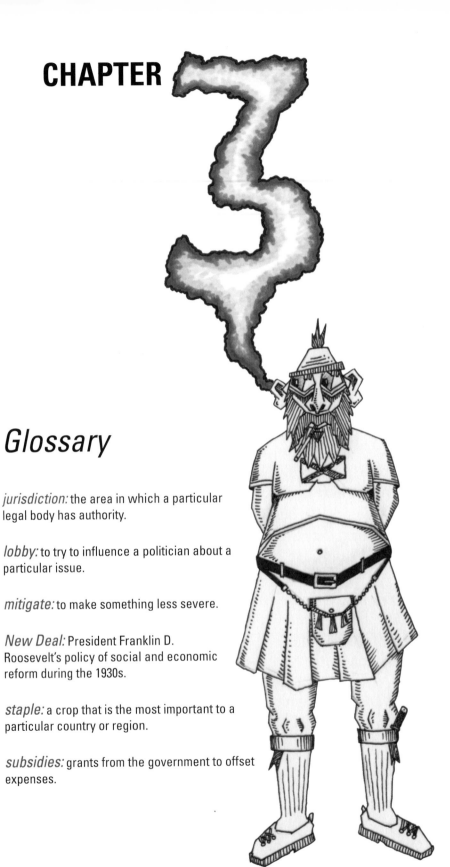

CHAPTER 3

Glossary

jurisdiction: the area in which a particular legal body has authority.

lobby: to try to influence a politician about a particular issue.

mitigate: to make something less severe.

New Deal: President Franklin D. Roosevelt's policy of social and economic reform during the 1930s.

staple: a crop that is the most important to a particular country or region.

subsidies: grants from the government to offset expenses.

Government and Tobacco: Laws and Bans

Tobacco laws that existed before 1964 did not address its safety. They focused on farming, marketing, and taxation. In fact, before 1965, the U.S. Department of Agriculture (USDA) conducted research on how to improve tobacco farming.

Early Regulations on Tobacco Farming
The 1933 Agricultural Adjustment Act
The 1930s was a decade of important agricultural legislation for tobacco farmers. The country was in the midst of the Great Depression, with plummeting prices for many goods

and services. President Franklin D. Roosevelt signed several laws as part of America's *New Deal*. One of them, the Agricultural Adjustment Act (AAA), was designed to stabilize prices for certain *staple* crops. Tobacco was one of them. That may seem odd now, but tobacco sales were very important to the country's economy.

The new law generated higher prices for crops by having farmers reduce production. To get farmers to plant less, an allotment plan was developed. Under the plan, only existing tobacco farmers with "allotments" from the USDA could grow this crop, and it could only be grown on the allotted acreage. For example, if a farmer had an allotment of fifteen acres (6 ha) for tobacco, he could not plant tobacco on more land than that. He could, however, rent that allotment to others. And allotments could be passed down to a person's descendants. Under the AAA, farmers were paid *subsidies* to leave fields barren.

The 1982 No Net Cost Tobacco Program Act

By the 1980s, many Americans and health organizations objected to using tax money to pay tobacco farmers. After all, it was now common knowledge that tobacco was responsible for numerous health problems. The No Net Cost Tobacco Program Act of 1982 prohibits tax-payer money from being used to pay tobacco subsidies. Instead, money to support the subsidies is raised by assessing a fee to both tobacco farmers and purchasers, and that money is used for the program.

The 1986 Tobacco Program Improvement Act

Four years later, the Tobacco Program Improvement Act was enacted. This act further curbed the tobacco subsidies first established by the 1933 Agricultural Adjustment Act. The 1986 act reduced minimum tobacco support prices and encouraged the selloff of the existing stockpile of tobacco. It also adjusted quotas by requiring that cigarette manufacturers tell the USDA a year in advance how much tobacco they wanted to purchase. The USDA uses that confidential information to establish quotas. The manufacturers must then purchase at least 90 percent of the amount they said they wanted.

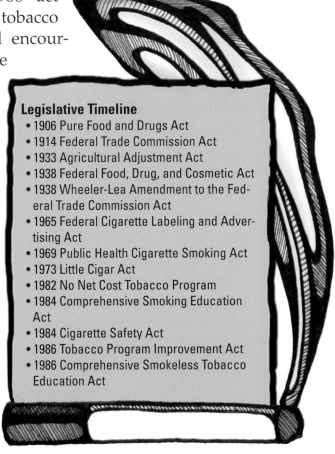

Legislative Timeline
- 1906 Pure Food and Drugs Act
- 1914 Federal Trade Commission Act
- 1933 Agricultural Adjustment Act
- 1938 Federal Food, Drug, and Cosmetic Act
- 1938 Wheeler-Lea Amendment to the Federal Trade Commission Act
- 1965 Federal Cigarette Labeling and Advertising Act
- 1969 Public Health Cigarette Smoking Act
- 1973 Little Cigar Act
- 1982 No Net Cost Tobacco Program
- 1984 Comprehensive Smoking Education Act
- 1984 Cigarette Safety Act
- 1986 Tobacco Program Improvement Act
- 1986 Comprehensive Smokeless Tobacco Education Act

The Food and Drug Administration and Tobacco

As the link between tobacco and health concerns became more widely recognized, the federal government knew that something had to be done about government subsidies for tobacco. Public opinion was shifting away from supporting the industry, but people who smoked and wanted to continue the habit did not want tobacco banned. The industry itself was among the nation's most profitable businesses. And it could afford to hire some of the best lawyers, scientists, and former government officials to *lobby* Congress on its behalf. Weighing these conflicting interests, the government decided to take steps to regulate tobacco.

The Pure Food and Drugs Act

The Pure Food and Drugs Act, passed in 1906, was the first federal law pertaining to foods and drugs. The act created the U.S. Food and Drug Administration (FDA) and gave this federal agency regulatory control over food and drugs. However, the law did not contain any reference to tobacco products. Drugs, as defined in the law, are those listed in the "U.S. Pharmacoepia or National Formulary." The inclusion of nicotine was con-

In 1906, the United States Congress passed the Pure Food and Drugs Act, which gave the FDA control over food and drugs, although this act excluded all tobacco products.

sidered when the law was drafted, but a lobbying effort by the tobacco industry succeeded in having it removed. Tobacco has been deliberately excluded from many laws governing such things as hazardous substances, chemical substances, and consumer products. A 1914 interpretation of the Pure Food and Drugs Act determined that the law should pertain to tobacco only when it is used to prevent, *mitigate*, or cure disease.

The 1938 Federal Food, Drug, and Cosmetic Act

For more than thirty years, the Pure Food and Drugs Act was the government's way of helping to maintain the safety of the products used by its citizens. But in 1938, another law went into effect that expanded the definition of drugs. The Federal Food, Drug, and Cosmetic Act (FFDCA) superseded the Pure Food and Drugs Act of 1906. Under the new law, a *drug* is defined as "articles intended for use in the diagnosis, cure, mitigation, treatment, or prevention of disease in man or other animals and articles (other than food) intended to affect the structure or any function of the body of man or other animals."

In 1953, the FDA successfully used FFDCA to assert its *jurisdiction* over Fairfax cigarettes. The FDA wasn't necessarily acting because smoking was dangerous. Rather, the FDA took action because of a medical claim by the manufacturer that Fairfax ciga-

Not Just About Smoking
It might seem as though Congress has concentrated solely on long-term health issues when considering legislation on smoking and tobacco. That's not true. In 1984, the Cigarette Safety Act was enacted to determine the commercial feasibility and technical possibility of creating cigarettes and little cigars that are less able to ignite mattresses and upholstery.

rettes could help prevent respiratory diseases, common colds, influenza, pneumonia, acute sinusitis, acute tonsillitis, scarlet fever, whooping cough, measles, meningitis, tuberculosis, mumps, middle-ear infections, and meningopneumonitis psittacosis (parrot fever).

In 1959, the FDA was again successful in using FFDCA against Trim Reducing-Aid cigarettes. Again, the FDA acted because of claims made by the manufacturer—in this case, the claim that the cigarettes could be used as a weight-reduction aid. According to package directions, the smoker should smoke one cigarette "shortly before meals . . . and whenever you are tempted to reach for a late evening snack."

The Federal Trade Commission and Tobacco

The Federal Trade Commission (FTC) is the government agency that regulates advertising. Established by the Federal Trade Commission Act of 1914, the FTC has regulatory authority over consumer product advertising in order to prevent deceptive and unfair acts and unlawful practices. The law requires truth in advertising, and it has been used to stop cigarette companies from making medical claims for their products.

For example, in 1942, the law was used to stop a manufacturer from saying Kool cigarettes protected users from catching colds. In 1950, the FTC stopped R. J. Reynolds from advertising that Camel cigarettes did not impair the endurance or physical condition of athletes, would never harm or irritate the throat, aided digestion, and were restful, soothing, and comforting to the nerves.

Only a couple of weeks after the surgeon general's 1964 report, the FTC proposed that health warnings be placed on cigarette packages and on cigarette ads. The FTC wanted the warnings to say that cigarette smok-

Before the development of the Federal Trade Commission, tobacco companies made claims in their ads that cigarettes could do things like improve digestion or soothe the nerves.

ing is dangerous to health and "may cause death from cancer or other diseases," but Congress stepped in and enacted a law before this rule could take effect.

Warning Labels

Congress has passed several laws requiring warning labels on cigarette packages. The first, the Federal Cigarette Labeling and Advertising Act, was passed in 1965. It required this watered down version of what the FTC wanted: "Caution: Cigarette smoking may be dangerous to your health." Despite the title of the law, it did not require warnings to be placed immediately on cigarette ads; in fact, it prohibited the FTC or other federal agencies from requiring them for three years. It did require the FTC to determine the effectiveness of the new warning label, to keep tabs on tobacco company advertising and other promotions, and then to make recommendations to Congress for future legislation. Congress also decided it wanted to receive annual reports on the health consequences of smoking from the Department of Health, Education, and Welfare and made that requirement part of the law. Additionally, the 1965 federal law prohibited states from issuing their own health warnings for cigarettes.

The Federal Communications Commission and Tobacco

The Federal Communications Commission (FCC) is an independent U.S. government agency, established in 1934, that is responsible for regulating interstate and international communications by radio, television, wire, satellite, and cable. In 1949, the FCC determined that television stations were "public trusts." According to the FCC, this meant that TV stations had an obligation to present contrasting points of view on controversial issues affecting the public. This policy became known as the Fairness Doctrine, and its goal was to ensure fair

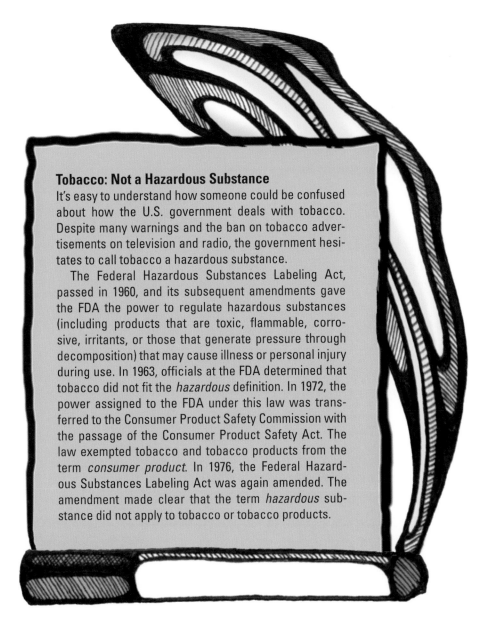

Tobacco: Not a Hazardous Substance

It's easy to understand how someone could be confused about how the U.S. government deals with tobacco. Despite many warnings and the ban on tobacco advertisements on television and radio, the government hesitates to call tobacco a hazardous substance.

The Federal Hazardous Substances Labeling Act, passed in 1960, and its subsequent amendments gave the FDA the power to regulate hazardous substances (including products that are toxic, flammable, corrosive, irritants, or those that generate pressure through decomposition) that may cause illness or personal injury during use. In 1963, officials at the FDA determined that tobacco did not fit the *hazardous* definition. In 1972, the power assigned to the FDA under this law was transferred to the Consumer Product Safety Commission with the passage of the Consumer Product Safety Act. The law exempted tobacco and tobacco products from the term *consumer product*. In 1976, the Federal Hazardous Substances Labeling Act was again amended. The amendment made clear that the term *hazardous* substance did not apply to tobacco or tobacco products.

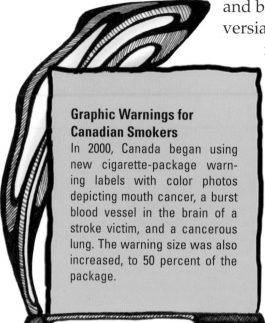

Graphic Warnings for Canadian Smokers

In 2000, Canada began using new cigarette-package warning labels with color photos depicting mouth cancer, a burst blood vessel in the brain of a stroke victim, and a cancerous lung. The warning size was also increased, to 50 percent of the package.

and balanced coverage of controversial issues. In 1967, the FCC ruled that the Fairness Doctrine, which was a policy rather than a law, applied to cigarette commercials. Some television and radio stations began to air warnings about the dangers of cigarette smoking, although they also continued broadcasting ads from tobacco companies.

Many stations did not comply with the Fairness Doctrine when it came to warnings about cigarettes, however. This led the FCC to push for a complete ban on cigarette commercials on television and radio. Meanwhile, the FTC was also still requesting a stronger health warning. In 1970, cigarette ads were banned on both television and radio when President Richard Nixon signed the Public Health Cigarette Smoking Act, which had passed in Congress the previous year. This law, which took effect on January 2, 1971, also required the warning on cigarette packages to be amended to make it clear that the warning came from the surgeon general (though it was still not as strong as the FTC wanted): "Warning: The Surgeon General Has Determined that Cigarette Smoking Is Dangerous to Your Health." Again, other health warnings were prohibited, and states were prevented from creating their own health-warning regulations or prohibitions against cigarette advertising. The surgeon general's warning also had to be placed on printed advertisements for cigarettes, though the FTC was prohibited from requiring them until March of 1972.

Cigarettes were the target of most of the initial tobacco-related laws. The laws did not address advertising of small cigars, which were also popular among smokers. This changed in 1973, when the Little Cigar Act added them to the list of tobacco products banned from advertising on radio and television.

The Surgeon General Speaks

As mentioned previously, warnings from the U.S. surgeon general have varied in strength since they first appeared. According to the 1984 Comprehensive Smoking Education Act, the following series of four health

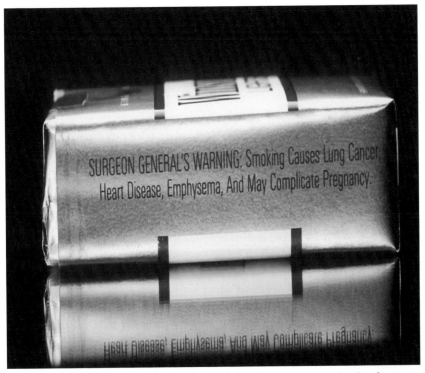

Now, alll cigarette packages sold in the United States are required to feature warning labels from the Surgeon General warning of the possible health effects of smoking.

warnings were to be rotated on cigarette packages and print advertising:

SURGEON GENERAL'S WARNING: Smoking Causes Lung Cancer, Heart Disease, Emphysema, and May Complicate Pregnancy.
SURGEON GENERAL'S WARNING: Quitting Smoking Now Greatly Reduces Serious Risks to Your Health.
SURGEON GENERAL'S WARNING: Smoking by Pregnant Women May Result in Fetal Injury, Premature Birth, and Low Birth Weight.
SURGEON GENERAL'S WARNING: Cigarette Smoke Contains Carbon Monoxide.

Despite the stronger warnings, the law still fell short of FTC recommendations. The FTC wanted the warnings to be more attention-grabbing. This law required the Centers for Disease Control and Prevention (CDC), which, like the FDA, is an agency operating under the Department of Health and Human Services (HHS), to collect, store, and analyze a confidential list of ingredients that are added to cigarettes and to prepare biennial reports on smoking and health for Congress.

The Law and Smokeless Tobacco

Some people believed that smokeless tobacco was a better tobacco-use alternative than smoking cigarettes and cigars. Baseball fans were often "treated" to televised close-ups of their favorite players chewing and spitting tobacco. One popular commercial of the time featured a well-known athlete touting his favorite brand and the benefits of "just a pinch between my cheek and gum."

In time, the health risks of smokeless tobacco became known. The federal government stepped in with the 1986 Comprehensive Smokeless Tobacco Education Act. The law required that the following warning labels be

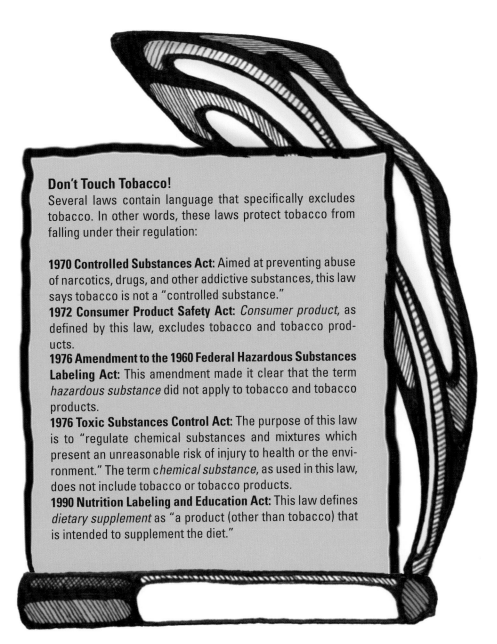

Don't Touch Tobacco!
Several laws contain language that specifically excludes tobacco. In other words, these laws protect tobacco from falling under their regulation:

1970 Controlled Substances Act: Aimed at preventing abuse of narcotics, drugs, and other addictive substances, this law says tobacco is not a "controlled substance."
1972 Consumer Product Safety Act: *Consumer product*, as defined by this law, excludes tobacco and tobacco products.
1976 Amendment to the 1960 Federal Hazardous Substances Labeling Act: This amendment made it clear that the term *hazardous substance* did not apply to tobacco and tobacco products.
1976 Toxic Substances Control Act: The purpose of this law is to "regulate chemical substances and mixtures which present an unreasonable risk of injury to health or the environment." The term c*hemical substance*, as used in this law, does not include tobacco or tobacco products.
1990 Nutrition Labeling and Education Act: This law defines *dietary supplement* as "a product (other than tobacco) that is intended to supplement the diet."

rotated on packages and advertisements for smokeless tobacco products:

WARNING: This product may cause mouth cancer.

WARNING: This product may cause gum disease and tooth loss.

WARNING: This product is not a safe alternative to cigarettes.

This time Congress agreed to the circle-and-arrow shape the FTC had earlier recommended for cigarettes. This law prohibited advertisements for smokeless tobacco on radio and television, and required the CDC to provide Congress with the same reports about smokeless tobacco as they do for cigarettes. Additionally, the Department of Health and Human Services must conduct a public education campaign on health hazards associated with smokeless tobacco use. It also required the FTC to prepare a report for Congress on the advertising, marketing, and sale of smokeless tobacco. Again, this law prohibited federal agencies and state governments from mandating other health warnings for these products.

From Smoke-Filled Rooms to Smoke-Free Airlines (and More)

Nonsmokers became concerned about exposure to secondhand smoke in the 1970s. One place where many felt especially vulnerable was on airplanes. Some people were already worried about breathing in recycled air, and being forced to breathe in tobacco smoke caused even more concern.

In 1973, the Civil Aeronautics Board required U.S. airlines to establish no-smoking sections on all commercial flights. In 1987, Public Law 100-202 banned smoking on domestic airline flights of two hours or less. In 1989, Public Law 101-164 banned it on flights scheduled for six hours or less. Smoking was banned on all domestic flights in 1990.

In 1976, regulations were passed to restrict smoking on American trains traveling on interstate routes. Smokers were confined to separate cars, and dining cars were made smoke-free. Bus passengers had to wait until 1990 for a similar ban. All passenger rail cars were made smoke-free in 2004.

The Pro-Children Act of 1994 banned smoking in public schools and in programs serving children that receive federal funding, such as community health centers, day care centers, and centers with Head Start programs.

President Bill Clinton issued an executive order making all federal workplaces smoke-free in 1997.

Though many government departments have a hand in regulating tobacco, the country's main consumer-product regulator—the FDA—has had limited authority when it comes to tobacco products. Many laws contain language that specifically excludes tobacco from regu-

Prior to 1997, smoking was allowed in offices and other public places. Now, however, all federal work-places have been declared smoke free.

lation. This doesn't mean that the FDA has sat by idly watching others deal with tobacco. FDA officials worked to determine how best to get tobacco under their jurisdiction. The intricate dance between the FDA and the tobacco industry began quietly at FDA headquarters and ended in the Supreme Court.

CHAPTER 4

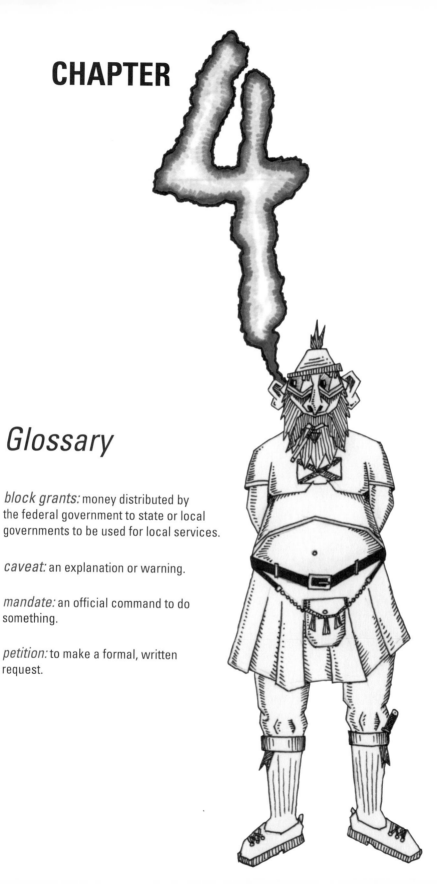

Glossary

block grants: money distributed by the federal government to state or local governments to be used for local services.

caveat: an explanation or warning.

mandate: an official command to do something.

petition: to make a formal, written request.

The FDA
Goes After
Tobacco

He didn't know it when he accepted the position of food and drug commissioner, but David Kessler's education and training as both a physician and a lawyer made him the perfect candidate to lead the FDA in its battle with the tobacco industry during the 1990s. The FDA's six-year odyssey against cigarette manufacturers involved undercover investigations, mysterious witnesses, political intrigue, and courtroom drama.

The FDA and Tobacco

The FDA has a huge mission. It enforces laws passed by Congress having to do with the foods we eat, the cosmetics we wear, the medicines we take, the medical devices used to help us when we're ill, the blood we receive via transfusions, and the packaged oxygen we breathe when our health demands it. But does the FDA have jurisdiction over cigarettes?

In 1977, Action on Smoking and Health (ASH), a nonprofit organization, *petitioned* the FDA to regulate cigarettes. The nonprofit believed that a cigarette was a drug and, as such, fell under the jurisdiction of the FDA. When the FDA (then led by Commissioner Donald Kennedy) turned down the organization's petition, ASH filed a lawsuit against the agency. The court found in the FDA's favor because no evidence had been presented to prove that cigarettes met the legal definition of a drug. However, the decision included a *caveat*: "Nothing in this opinion should suggest that the Administration is irrevocably bound by any long-standing interpretations. . . . An administrative agency is clearly free to revise its interpretations." In other words, the decision did not prevent the FDA from revising its opinion about whether it had the authority to regulate tobacco in the future. Citizen's action groups, including one called the Coalition on Smoking or Health, ramped up their efforts to try to convince the FDA to revise its policy and regulate tobacco.

The phrase "not including tobacco or tobacco products" appears in many laws regulating drugs. The Federal Food, Drug, and Cosmetic Act (FFDCA) does not contain this language. Remember, according to the FFDCA, drugs are "articles intended for use in the diagnosis, cure, mitigation, treatment, or prevention of disease in man or other animals and articles (other than food) intended to affect the structure of any function of the body."

In 1977, the FDA determined that cigarettes were not a drug and therefore could not be monitored by the FDA. However, this changed in the mid-1990s and now tobacco is considered a drug.

Whistle-Blower Heroes

To protect the identity of people who supplied valuable information about the inner workings of Big Tobacco, the FDA used code names so they would remain anonymous. Later, many revealed their identities. Meet a few of them:

"Bio": a scientist who previously worked for Philip Morris and told the FDA about electroencephalography (EEG) tests the company conducted to determine how cigarette smoke affects the human brain.

"Cigarette": Victor DeNoble, a psychologist and former Philip Morris researcher.

"Cigarette Jr.": Paul Mele, a former Philip Morris research scientist. He and DeNoble conducted research on rats and submitted a paper on their findings to the journal *Psychopharmacology* in 1983. Philip Morris forced them to withdraw the paper and said, "The data you're generating are inconsistent with our position in lawsuits." In 1984, they were directed to kill all the research animals they had used, and then they were fired.

"Deep Cough": a former R. J. Reynolds employee who provided details about the company's manufacturing process. He also revealed industry secrets while disguised in a television interview on ABC's Day One program in 1994.

"Macon": a scientist for Brown & Williamson who revealed that Y-1 tobacco—a genetically engineered high-nicotine tobacco—had been grown in Brazil. The FDA later discovered that it had also been grown experimentally in the United States.

"PC": a former product developer for Brown & Williamson. He explained that, in 1991, after receiving complaints of an odd taste in their product, Brown & Williamson ordered groups of employees to smoke cigarettes laced with various chemicals in an effort to determine which was responsible for the offending flavor. More than thirty solvents were used in the test.

"Research": Jeffrey Wigand, a biochemist and former Brown & Williamson vice president for research. He revealed industry efforts to genetically engineer high-nicotine tobacco, code named Y-1. Wigand's story was the subject of a 1999 movie titled The Insider, starring Russell Crowe and Al Pacino.

"Saint": a chemical engineer who had worked for Philip Morris. She revealed that Philip Morris had asked her to conduct an experiment to remove specified carcinogens from tobacco; the experiment was successful.

In his book, *A Question of Intent: A Great American Battle with a Deadly Industry*, Dr. David Kessler recalls his unscheduled meeting with David Adams, an FDA employee working in the agency's policy office. Adams explained that other FDA employees had determined that it was possible for cigarette manufacturers to remove nicotine from their cigarettes, but instead, they had chosen to leave it in. Did this mean that they "intended" for the nicotine in cigarettes to addict smokers to tobacco products? Did this mean the FDA could claim jurisdiction over cigarettes? Dr. Kessler decided the FDA needed to discover the intention of the tobacco companies.

Building a Case

The FDA assembled a team to determine if nicotine was a drug and therefore fell under the FDA's jurisdiction. FDA officials wanted to know what tobacco companies knew about the addictive qualities of nicotine and when they knew it. They wanted to know if cigarette manufacturers deliberately used nicotine because of its addictive qualities and the physiological effects it has on the brain. They began to do research and collect evidence. Fortunately, they had someone on the "inside" working with them.

Enter a Whistle-Blower

"Deep Cough," a former R. J. Reynolds employee, supplied the FDA with enough information for the agency to move forward. He had the inside knowledge necessary to provide the FDA with details of the tobacco maker's manufacturing methods. He told the agency that tobacco companies manipulated nicotine levels in cigarettes as a way to keep smokers hooked.

Based on the information provided by Deep Cough in 1994, those at the FDA believed they had the information necessary to expand their investigation. Kessler sent a letter to the Coalition on Smoking or Health, saying that if the agency could prove intent, it would consider regulating tobacco. During the investigation that followed, a series of whistle-blowers supplied information on how cigarettes are made, the industry's knowledge of nicotine's addictive qualities, secret patents aimed at developing genetically engineered high-nicotine tobacco, how tobacco leaves are blended to produce desired nicotine levels, and so on. Sometimes an informant provided details outright; other times only clues were offered. Often, industry employees must sign confidentiality agreements as a condition of employment. Some whistle-blowers wanted to help the FDA but were afraid of losing their jobs, benefits, and pensions if they violated those agreements. In those cases, they were less forthcoming but often tried to steer investigators in the direction of important information.

Tobacco Companies and Manipulation

The FDA collected thousands of pages of evidence showing that tobacco companies recognized the importance of nicotine to cigarettes. An R. J. Reynolds report issued in 1991 stated,

> We are basically in the nicotine business. . . . It is in the best long term interest for [R. J. Reynolds] to be able to control and effectively utilize every pound of nicotine we purchase. Effective control of nicotine in our products should equate to a significant product performance and cost advantage.

But R. J. Reynolds wasn't the only target. An envelope mailed anonymously to the FDA disclosed "Root Technology," the code name for a secret Brown & Williamson project that entailed using ammonia to manipulate nicotine by increasing its potency.

FDA Labs Conduct Their Own Tests

The FDA tested several cigarette brands, and their tests yielded some surprising results. For example, of the ten cigarettes manufactured

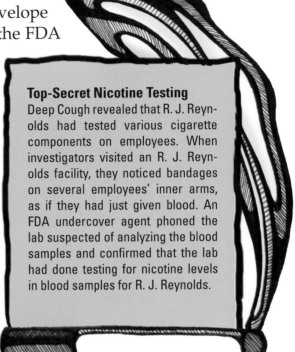

Top-Secret Nicotine Testing

Deep Cough revealed that R. J. Reynolds had tested various cigarette components on employees. When investigators visited an R. J. Reynolds facility, they noticed bandages on several employees' inner arms, as if they had just given blood. An FDA undercover agent phoned the lab suspected of analyzing the blood samples and confirmed that the lab had done testing for nicotine levels in blood samples for R. J. Reynolds.

by one company, the "low-tar" cigarette had the highest nicotine content, just the opposite of what might have been expected. The industry had claimed that nicotine levels "followed tar levels." In other words, if tar were reduced, nicotine would also be reduced. Dr. Kessler requested data from the FTC, which had collected these statistics from the cigarette industry. The data showed that when tar levels went down, nicotine levels went up. To the FDA, this indicated that manufacturers were deliberately manipulating nicotine levels.

Congress Holds Hearings

U.S. Representatives Henry Waxman (D–California) and Mike Synar (D–Oklahoma), had tried to enact antismoking legislation, including Synar's proposed amendment that required states receiving federal funding in the form of *block grants* to enforce laws against minors purchasing cigarettes. After the FDA decided to broaden its jurisdiction to include tobacco, Waxman and Synar called for Congressional hearings to better understand the agency's reasoning for this shift.

Testimony

The CEOs of major tobacco companies were called to testify, but instead of appearing themselves, they sent

PRIVILEGED AND CONFIDENTIAL
Produced as required by the Court's March 7, 1998 Order in
State of Minnesota, et al. v. Philip Morris, et al.
Court File No.: C1-94-8565

DRAFT -- 7/9/90

Statement of Charles O. Whitley

on behalf of

The Tobacco Institute

before the

Subcommittee on Health and the Environment
Committee on Energy and Commerce
U.S. House of Representatives

July 12, 1990

Mr. Chairman, distinguished members of the Subcommittee and former colleagues, I appreciate this opportunity to testify on H.R. 5041, the "Tobacco Control and Health Protection Act."

H.R. 5041 would repeal the Federal Cigarette Labeling and Advertising Act, Sec. 3 of the Comprehensive Smoking Education Act and the Comprehensive Smokeless Tobacco Health Education Act of 1986. In place of that statutory framework, H.R. 5041 would --

· severely restrict the content of cigarette advertisements and ban promotional activities, making brand advertising effectively impossible;

· require cigarette packages and advertisements to carry a series of "scare" warnings and otherwise serve as vehicles for government antismoking messages;

· invite state and local governments to attempt to ban or restrict such cigarette advertising as would continue to be permitted under the bill;

TIMN 0032095

Big tobacco companies sent Charles Whitley to testify against the regulation of tobacco by the FDA.

Charles Whitley, head of the Tobacco Institute and a former congressman, to represent them. The industry may have hoped that Whitley would be able to convince his former colleagues in Congress to reject the FDA's proposal to regulate tobacco. Some sitting members of Congress—particularly those from tobacco-producing states or with ties to Big Tobacco—refused to participate in or support the hearings. Congressman Thomas J. Bliley Jr. (R–Virginia), the ranking minority member on the House Oversight and Investigations Committee, called Dr. Kessler's move to assert FDA jurisdiction over tobacco "precipitous and reckless" then left the hearings before Dr. Kessler presented any testimony.

In his opening statement, Dr. Kessler testified:

Seventeen million [smokers] try to quit each year but for every one who quits, at least nine try and fail. Three out of four adult smokers say they are addicted. . . . Some of today's cigarettes may in fact qualify as high-technology nicotine delivery systems that deliver nicotine in quantities sufficient to create and sustain addiction.

In discussing industry patents, Dr. Kessler said, "The research undertaken by the cigarette industry is more and more resembling drug development."

He went on to explain the results of FDA tests and FTC data that showed that

How Big Is Big Tobacco?
One R. J. Reynolds cigarette-production facility inspected by FDA investigators covered approximately 46 acres (18.5 ha) and used the same amount of power as 56,000 houses. It was so large that many employees used bicycles within the building to get from one area to another.

The FDA received criticism from all sides for its proposed regulation of tobacco.
In the end, they were forced to compromise and settle for restricting the sale of
tobacco to all minors.

increased nicotine in a cigarette accompanied decreased tar, and the importance of the word *intent* as it is used in the Federal Food, Drug, and Cosmetic Act.

Several committee members asked questions, including Chairman Waxman, who wanted to get information on the record. Summarizing some of Dr. Kessler's testimony, Congressman Waxman said, "In other words, the tobacco industry sponsored studies on their own where they found out that nicotine was addictive and before the public could know about it, they acted to suppress those studies?" Dr. Kessler told him that was correct.

Seven tobacco industry CEOs and several industry researchers did show up at a subsequent hearing to respond to Dr. Kessler's previous testimony. An R. J. Reynolds representative testified that he didn't know whether smoking caused cancer. A representative of Lorillard said he didn't believe smoking caused cancer. Someone from Philip Morris testified, "We don't know what causes cancer, in general, right now." Six CEOs testified that they did not believe nicotine is addictive. A seventh said, "Cigarettes and nicotine clearly do not meet the classic definition of addiction. There is no intoxication."

A Widespread Attack Against the FDA

Congressmen Waxman and Bliley's roles on the committee reversed when the Republican party took over Congress after the November 1994 election. Congressman Bliley had close ties to the tobacco industry, and he announced almost immediately that he saw no need for further hearings. In his view, there was no reason for further regulation of tobacco.

Congressman Newt Gingrich, the new Speaker of the House, called Dr. Kessler a "bully and a thug" on national television. Organizations critical of the FDA suggested that the agency be dismantled. When the FDA refused to turn over information on its confidential sources to the Congressional Committee, some Republican committee members asked the General Accounting Office to conduct a review of the agency and its practices and to consider filing criminal charges against the FDA. Kentucky Republican Jim Bunning said of the FDA, "It's a rogue agency that's out of control and Congress needs to slap it down."

What to Do

At the first congressional hearing, Dr. Kessler had acknowledged that FDA jurisdiction over tobacco could have far-reaching consequences:

> It could lead to the possible removal of nicotine-containing cigarettes from the market, the limiting of the amount of nicotine in cigarettes to levels that are not addictive, or restricting access to them, unless the industry could show that nicotine-containing cigarettes are safe and effective.

He concluded, "On these issues we seek guidance from Congress."

Ultimately, the FDA did not seek those far-reaching restrictions. Instead it settled for a much more modest proposal. FDA officials decided to consider smoking as a pediatric disease (since most smokers begin the habit before they are twenty years old) and treat cigarettes as they do medical devices. The FDA would not ban cigarettes. Instead, the agency would restrict their availability and use by young people under age eighteen. The Department of Justice reviewed the FDA proposal for jurisdiction and agreed with it. President Bill Clinton agreed. Publication of the final rule was announced in 1996; Dr. Kessler resigned from the FDA shortly after that. But if the FDA and the government thought things were settled, they were mistaken. The tobacco companies were ready to launch an almost immediate challenge to the FDA's new authority.

Tobacco Fights Back

Round One: FDA

Tobacco companies filed their case in the Greensboro, North Carolina, U.S. District Court—in the heart of tobacco-growing country. The companies claimed that

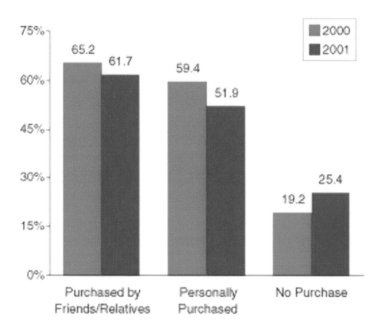

This graph indicates that the FDA's restrictions on tobacco sales may be reducing young adults' tobacco consumption. Not all experts, however, agree that these modest reductions are enough.

High Court Doesn't Nix FDA Oversight of All Nicotine

Although the Supreme Court said no to FDA regulation of cigarettes, the agency does have jurisdiction over other nicotine-delivery products, including nicotine gum, patches, and inhalers.

the FDA did not have congressional authority to regulate tobacco and that tobacco did not fit the legal definition of either a drug or a medical device. Judge William Osteen presided over the 1997 hearing and laid out the three main questions he would be deciding. In simple terms, he wanted to know:

Whether Congress had ever intended for the FDA to have jurisdiction over tobacco.

If the FDA was correct in classifying tobacco products as drugs, devices, or a combination of the two.

If the regulations the FDA proposed lay within its *mandate*.

Two months later, Judge Osteen issued a decision in favor of the FDA, with one exception. He ruled that the FDA had no authority to require tobacco companies to limit advertising that could influence minors.

Round Two: Tobacco

Both sides appealed the decision. The U.S. Court of Appeals in Charleston, West Virginia, heard the case in 1998. The three judges who heard the case voted 2 to 1 against the FDA.

Round Three: The Supreme Court

FDA v. Brown & Williamson et al. reached the Supreme Court in December 1999, and the justices reached their 5-to-4 decision in April 2000. Justice Stephen Breyer read the dissent. The dissenting justices agreed with the FDA argument that nicotine is a drug and should fall under FDA jurisdiction. But a majority of the justices believed Congress, not the FDA, had authority over tobacco. Justice Sandra Day O'Connor summarized the majority opinion. She admitted that smoking is "one of the most troubling public health problems facing our nation today" and "poses perhaps the single most significant threat to public health in the United States." But

The FDA considered tobacco a pediatric disease and started campaigns to stop the spread of underage smoking.

the majority of the justices believed that in order for the FDA to exert jurisdiction over tobacco, Congress would have to pass a law giving the agency that power. The majority decision said Congress "has clearly precluded the FDA from asserting jurisdiction to regulate tobacco

In 2000, the FDA passed a law forbidding tobacco companies from sponsoring sports events; they used the logic that this influenced many young people to start smoking because of the widespread presence of cigarette products.

products." They went on to say that FDA jurisdiction over tobacco was "inconsistent with the intent that Congress has expressed in the [Federal Food, Drug, and Cosmetic Act's] overall regulatory scheme and in the tobacco-specific legislation that it has enacted subsequent to the [FFDCA]."

After that decision, a bill was introduced in Congress that would give the FDA the authority to regulate tobacco. However, the tobacco lobby strenuously opposed it, and the bill was defeated.

FDA officials wanted to forbid the tobacco industry from using cartoon characters and only allow black and white text to advertise cigarettes in magazines and on billboards. They also wanted to stop product promotions that placed cigarette names on T-shirts and baseball caps. Despite the Supreme Court ruling, those prohibitions did go into effect. Tobacco companies could no longer sell cigarettes in "kiddie packs" or be part of giveaways. Vending-machine, self-service, and mail-order sales of cigarettes would end, and cigarette brand names could no longer be used when sponsoring sporting events.

How could this have happened, since the FDA lost its court battle? The answer lies in something called the Master Settlement Agreement, as we shall see in chapter 5.

CHAPTER 5

Glossary

advocacy: active support for a cause.

antitrust: in opposition to trusts or cartels that create monopolies in order to make unfair profits.

class-action cases: legal actions brought by an individual or group representing others who experienced the same legal problem.

escrow: money or property given to a person but held by a third party until specific conditions are met.

States and Tobacco: Let's Make a Deal

Many people who smoked and then suffered health consequences began filing lawsuits against the manufacturers of
their cigarette brands. "Personal choice" was a major defense
tobacco companies had been using in these cases, and they had
been winning. But information uncovered by FDA investigators soon became public knowledge. Now that the public was
beginning to understand that smokers had become addicted
to the nicotine in cigarettes, and that the industry knew this
would happen but had kept it secret, how would judges and
juries rule in the lawsuits that were certain to be filed?

Tobacco's First Loss

Cigarette manufacturers initially won their cases in court. But that winning streak was about to come to an end. When the seven industry CEOs testified before Congress that nicotine wasn't addictive, Grady Carter was watching their declarations on television. After losing a lung to cancer, Grady had finally been able to end his addiction after forty-three years. Grady's smoking habit had begun almost by accident: When he was just a kid, he discovered a pack of cigarettes on a fencepost on his family's farm and smoked one. After that, he finished off butts left lying around by his uncles. By the time he was seventeen, Grady was a regular smoker of Lucky Strikes. Beginning in the 1960s and continuing for almost thirty years, Grady struggled to break the habit.

Grady decided to sue Brown & Williamson, the maker of Lucky Strikes. Attorney Norwood Wilner took the

The MSA limited how tobacco companies could advertise their products, including banning the use of logo merchandise and advertising at events that were mainly attended by minors.

case, which was the first in a series of cases he planned to launch against tobacco companies. *Carter v. Brown & Williamson* was filed in Florida.

Documents provided by a man named Merrell Williams were important evidence in the case. While working as a paralegal, Merrell Williams had seen documents belonging to Brown & Williamson, a client of the law firm where he worked. Williams, a smoker whose preferred brand was manufactured by Brown & Williamson, decided to make photocopies of these documents for himself. The documents indicated that the manufacturer had known that nicotine was addictive and smoking was a health hazard since the 1960s; Brown & Williamson had stopped trying to develop a safer cigarette.

After just ten hours of deliberation, the jury found in Grady's favor and awarded him $750,000. Not surprisingly, Brown & Williamson appealed. When the Florida Appeals Court overturned the decision, the case went to the Florida Supreme Court. In 2000, that court reinstated the judgment in Grady's favor. Brown & Williamson tried to take the case to the U.S. Supreme Court, but the high court refused to hear it. Thus, Grady Carter became the first person to beat Big Tobacco; he ultimately received $1.1 million (the original damages plus interest).

States Go After Tobacco

At the same time that individuals were filing lawsuits against tobacco companies, the financial burden of increasing Medicaid costs due to tobacco-related illnesses was fueling an assault against Big Tobacco by the states. Many *class-action cases* were being filed against tobacco companies. Fearful of years of endless—and expensive—litigation and the huge payouts that were beginning to accrue, four major tobacco companies (Brown & Williamson, Lorillard, Philip Morris, and R. J. Reynolds) began negotiating a compromise with state attorneys general. In late 1998, a compromise called the Master Settlement Agreement (MSA) was reached

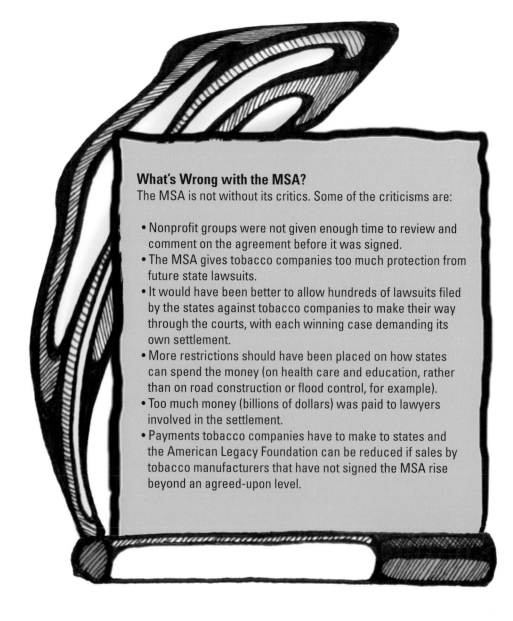

What's Wrong with the MSA?
The MSA is not without its critics. Some of the criticisms are:

- Nonprofit groups were not given enough time to review and comment on the agreement before it was signed.
- The MSA gives tobacco companies too much protection from future state lawsuits.
- It would have been better to allow hundreds of lawsuits filed by the states against tobacco companies to make their way through the courts, with each winning case demanding its own settlement.
- More restrictions should have been placed on how states can spend the money (on health care and education, rather than on road construction or flood control, for example).
- Too much money (billions of dollars) was paid to lawyers involved in the settlement.
- Payments tobacco companies have to make to states and the American Legacy Foundation can be reduced if sales by tobacco manufacturers that have not signed the MSA rise beyond an agreed-upon level.

The use of cartoon characters to advertise cigarette products was also banned by the MSA settlement.

with forty-six states. (A settlement of more than $35 billion had already been reached with Florida, Minnesota, Mississippi, and Texas.) Six U.S. territories or districts (American Samoa, the District of Columbia, Guam, the Northern Mariana Islands, Puerto Rico, and U.S. Virgin Islands) were also part of the MSA, and forty other tobacco companies signed on later. To compensate for health costs stemming from tobacco use, tobacco companies agreed to pay the states more than $240 billion over the next twenty-five years, with different states receiving different amounts. Each state could spend the money however it wished. Taken as a whole, this was the largest civil settlement in history.

The MSA is a complicated settlement. No changes can be made to the MSA unless all parties agree. Among other agreed-upon points, in order to limit youth access to their products, tobacco companies agreed to ban:

- the use of cartoon characters in advertising.
- billboards and other large signs advertising tobacco products in stadiums and arenas, transit areas, video arcades, and shopping malls. (Tobacco companies may place poster-sized ads in video arcades, shopping malls, arenas, and stadiums.)
- tobacco-brand-logo merchandise such as T-shirts, baseball caps, and backpacks (except at certain events sponsored by tobacco companies).
- free product sampling anywhere (except enclosed areas where no minors are present).
- payments for use of cigarettes in movies, television programs, live recorded performances, videos, and video games (this practice is known as product placement).
- brand-name sponsorship of concerts, team sports, and events where youth make up a significant portion of the audience. (An exception was made to allow Brown & Williamson to sponsor either the Kool Jazz Festival or the GPC Country Music Festival. Corporations can sponsor athletic, music, art, cultural, and social events.)
- sponsorship of events where minors are contestants or paid participants.

More Concessions

Additionally, tobacco companies agreed to limit themselves to one brand-name sponsorship each year. They also agreed to eliminate small cigarette packs, which might have greater appeal to young people, by selling a minimum of twenty cigarettes per package until December 2001. After that, states would have to enact their own legislation if they wished to continue the ban.

State and local lobbying efforts by tobacco companies are also restricted under the MSA. For example, if states do opt to pass laws extending the ban on small cigarette packages, tobacco companies agreed not to lobby against those proposed laws. Likewise, they cannot lobby against state or local laws that place limits on

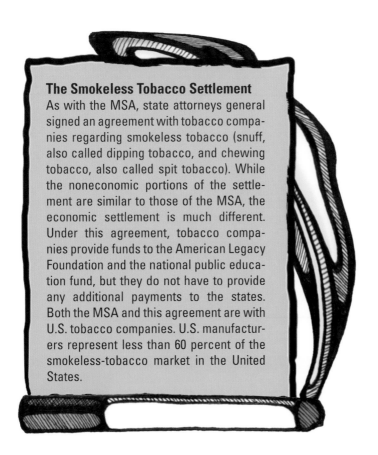

The Smokeless Tobacco Settlement
As with the MSA, state attorneys general signed an agreement with tobacco companies regarding smokeless tobacco (snuff, also called dipping tobacco, and chewing tobacco, also called spit tobacco). While the noneconomic portions of the settlement are similar to those of the MSA, the economic settlement is much different. Under this agreement, tobacco companies provide funds to the American Legacy Foundation and the national public education fund, but they do not have to provide any additional payments to the states. Both the MSA and this agreement are with U.S. tobacco companies. U.S. manufacturers represent less than 60 percent of the smokeless-tobacco market in the United States.

The Cigarette Advertising and Promotion Code: A Tobacco Industry "Voluntary" Code of Conduct

This code was superseded by the MSA:

- Cigarette advertising shall not appear in publications directed primarily to those under 21 years of age, including school, college, or university media (such as athletic, theatrical or other programs), comic books or comic supplements.
- No one depicted in cigarette advertising shall be or appear to be under 25 years of age.
- Cigarette advertising shall not suggest that smoking is essential to social prominence, distinction, success, or sexual attraction, nor shall it picture a person smoking in an exaggerated manner.
- Cigarette advertising may picture attractive, healthy-looking people, provided there is no implication that their attractiveness and good health are due to cigarette smoking.
- Cigarette advertising shall not depict as a smoker anyone who is or has been well known as an athlete, nor shall it show any smoker participating in, or obviously just having participated in, a physical activity requiring stamina or athletic conditioning beyond that of normal recreation.
- No sports or celebrity testimonials shall be used or those of others who would have special appeal to persons under 21 years of age.

(*Source*: Reynolds American Inc. http://www.reynoldsamerican.com/Governance/conduct_V.aspx)

Cigarette ads like this one, which portrays people participating in a strenuous physical activity, were banned by the MSA.

access to vending machines or prohibit sales of nonto-bacco products designed to look like cigarettes or cigars, such as candy or bubble gum.

Tobacco companies also agreed to dissolve trade associations. The Center for Indoor Air Research (CIAR), the Council for Indoor Air Research (CIAR), and the Tobacco Institute were all disbanded, but the MSA required that their records relating to lawsuits be preserved. The agreement also required industry research and other records to be made public.

The MSA led to the creation of the American Legacy Foundation (ALF), an antismoking *advocacy* organization, in 1999. Each year ALF spends $100 million on the "Truth Campaign," a nationwide advertising effort aimed at bringing facts about tobacco to young adults and teens.

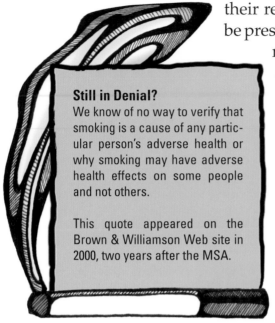

Still in Denial?
We know of no way to verify that smoking is a cause of any particular person's adverse health or why smoking may have adverse health effects on some people and not others.

This quote appeared on the Brown & Williamson Web site in 2000, two years after the MSA.

Finally, tobacco companies agreed to end several legal challenges they had launched against states.

What did tobacco companies gain from signing the MSA? State governments were prohibited from bringing future lawsuits against the industry to recover health care costs or for fraud or *antitrust* issues.

Where Does the Money Come From?

The money used to make MSA payments comes from cigarette sales and is tax-deductible for tobacco companies. Each time someone purchases cigarettes, a portion of the payment eventually goes to pay the states. Tobacco companies can then deduct that amount from the income they took in that year.

What about Tobacco Companies That Didn't Sign the MSA?

Companies that did not sign the MSA are still subject to state lawsuits. Additionally, they have to put money into an *escrow* account. If a state decides to bring a lawsuit against one of these companies, the money in escrow can be used to pay a settlement.

Even though the FDA was denied jurisdiction over tobacco, many of the concessions they wanted to place on manufacturers went into effect when the MSA was signed. While the FDA was attempting to gain jurisdiction over tobacco, the Department of Justice (DOJ) began its own investigation. The DOJ spent five years determining if tobacco representatives had lied about nicotine manipulation to the FDA and when they testified before Congress. Then the department went to court.

CHAPTER 6

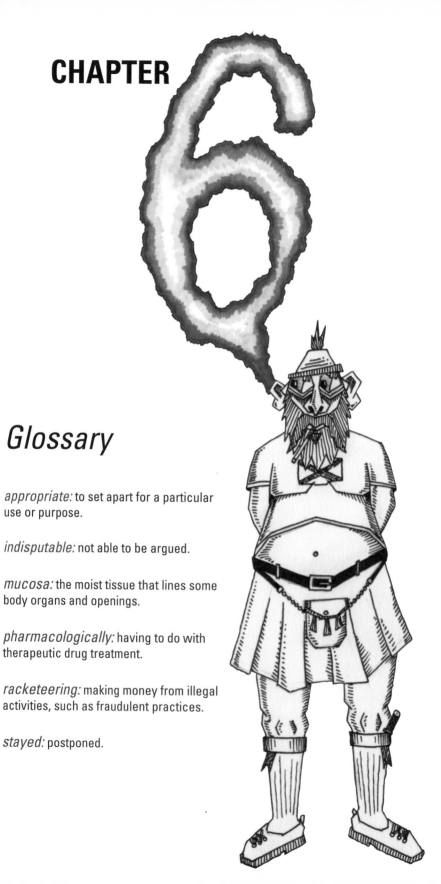

Glossary

appropriate: to set apart for a particular use or purpose.

indisputable: not able to be argued.

mucosa: the moist tissue that lines some body organs and openings.

pharmacologically: having to do with therapeutic drug treatment.

racketeering: making money from illegal activities, such as fraudulent practices.

stayed: postponed.

The DOJ
Takes on
Tobacco

The Honorable Gladys Kessler of the U.S. District Court for the District of Columbia (no relation to FDA Commissioner David Kessler) presided over *United States of America v. Philip Morris USA Inc., et al.*, a civil case filed in 1999. The case arose as the Department of Justice (DOJ) accused ten tobacco companies of *racketeering*. According to the DOJ, the defendants conspired to conceal information concerning the health consequences of smoking and to mislead and defraud the public. The companies and organizations charged in the suit were:

• American Tobacco Company, which merged with Brown & Williamson and is now part of Reynolds American

- B.A.T. Industries p.l.c., now part of BATCo, British American Tobacco (Investments) Ltd.
- Brown & Williamson Tobacco Co., now part of Reynolds American
- Lorillard Tobacco Company
- Philip Morris Companies, now Altria
- Philip Morris, Inc., now Philip Morris USA, Inc.
- R. J. Reynolds Tobacco Co., now Reynolds American
- The Council for Tobacco Research—U.S.A., Inc
- The Liggett Group, Inc.
- The Tobacco Institute, Inc.

In 1999, ten different tobacco companies were sued for allegedly keeping information from the public about the possible health effects of smoking.

Case Background

In January 1999, President Bill Clinton gave his State of the Union address. In the address, the president said the federal government would bring a civil case against tobacco companies. The Clinton administration charged that tobacco companies had committed fraud by concealing health information about smoking from the public since the 1950s. The govern-

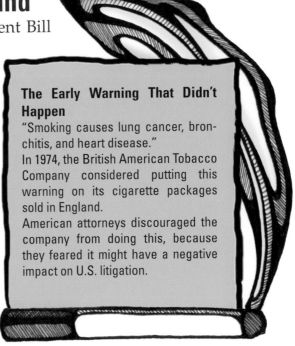

The Early Warning That Didn't Happen

"Smoking causes lung cancer, bronchitis, and heart disease."

In 1974, the British American Tobacco Company considered putting this warning on its cigarette packages sold in England.

American attorneys discouraged the company from doing this, because they feared it might have a negative impact on U.S. litigation.

ment wanted to recover some of the $25 billion it was spending each year treating smoking-related illnesses.

Republicans in Congress refused to *appropriate* the $20 million necessary for the DOJ to pursue the case, so the administration obtained the money through budgetary changes in various departments. The case went forward, but in 2000 Judge Kessler dismissed the part of the suit relating to recovery of health care costs. The racketeering portion of the case continued, and testimony began in 2004. There were 247 witnesses.

The Judge's Decision

In 2006, Judge Kessler ruled that the defendants had violated civil provisions of the Racketeer Influenced and Corrupt Organizations Act (RICO). In her findings,

Judge Kessler said that beginning at least by 1953 and extending at least until the year 2000, tobacco companies

> mounted a coordinated, well-financed, sophisticated public relations campaign to attack and distort the scientific evidence demonstrating the relationship between smoking and disease, claiming that the link between the two was still an "open question." Finally, in doing so, they ignored the massive documentation in their internal corporate files from their own scientists, executives, and public relations people.

Judge Kessler argued that tobacco companies were not being honest about the fact that cigarettes can cause heart disease and other serious health problems.

Judge Kessler also said the defendants falsely denied that they could control nicotine. According to Judge Kessler, tobacco companies do manipulate nicotine levels, and they do so to "create and sustain addiction." Judge Kessler found:

Defendants have added ammonia compounds in order to enhance consumer use of cigarettes by: (1) increasing the amount of nicotine that is transferred from the tobacco to the smoke; (2) improving the sensory response to nicotine in the mouth and oral *mucosa*; and (3) increasing the speed of delivery of nicotine to the bloodstream and possibly to the brain.

According to Judge Kessler, Colin Greig, a product developer for British American Tobacco, once described tobacco as "a fast, highly *pharmacologically* effective and cheap 'drug' contained within a 'relatively cheap and efficient delivery system.'" That "delivery system," was the cigarette.

Consequences

The government had sought damages to pay for a smoking-cessation program and an antismoking advertising program aimed at young people. Judge Kessler did not order the defendants to pay damages, but did order them to discontinue using terms such as *light* and *ultra light* to market cigarettes.

The defendants filed an appeal with the U.S. Circuit Court of Appeals for the District of Columbia. That court *stayed* the remedies ordered by Judge Kessler until an appeal could be heard.

What about Secondhand Smoke?

Judge Kessler said, "Internally, defendants recognized that ETS [environmental tobacco smoke] is hazardous to nonsmokers," and "Most importantly, research funded by Defendants themselves provided evidence confirming the public health authorities' warnings that non-smokers' exposure to cigarette smoke was a health hazard." Judge Kessler found that tobacco companies had made promises to the public

> intended to deceive the American public into believing that there was no risk associated with passive smoking and that the Defendants would fund objective research to find definitive answers. Instead, over the decades that followed, Defendants took steps to undermine independent research, to fund research designed and controlled to generate industry-favorable results, and to suppress adverse research results.

The judge further found that tobacco companies made misleading and even false statements denying the danger of secondhand smoke, and that they continue to obscure "the fact that ETS is hazardous to nonsmokers."

A Look Back at Secondhand Smoke

The Environmental Protection Agency (EPA) designated ETS (also known as secondhand smoke or passive smoke) a class A carcinogen in 1992. The agency had already made the declaration on a tentative basis in 1990. This classification indicates that ETS has achieved the agency's highest level of scientific certainty that it causes cancer. According to the EPA, secondhand smoke

Secondhand smoke can be just as dangerous as actually smoking a cigarette; this is especially true for children whose parents smoke and who are constantly exposed to the chemicals in the smoke.

The effects of second hand smoke on children, in a public service ad targeted to parents.

in the United States is one of most important environmental risks people face and is responsible for approximately 3,000 lung cancer deaths each year among nonsmokers.

The tobacco industry's response to the EPA designation of ETS as a class A carcinogen was to file a lawsuit against the EPA in 1993. Evidence made public in another case showed that the Tobacco Institute (which was disbanded

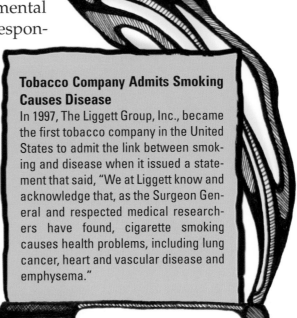

Tobacco Company Admits Smoking Causes Disease
In 1997, The Liggett Group, Inc., became the first tobacco company in the United States to admit the link between smoking and disease when it issued a statement that said, "We at Liggett know and acknowledge that, as the Surgeon General and respected medical researchers have found, cigarette smoking causes health problems, including lung cancer, heart and vascular disease and emphysema."

in 1998), in cooperation with two law firms, headed a project that ultimately paid a total of $156,000 to thirteen scientists for submitting letters critical of the EPA report to influential publications. In 1998, the judge in Big Tobacco's case against the EPA ruled that some parts of the EPA report were not valid. The EPA appealed the decision to a higher court, and in 2002, the three judges in the Fourth U.S. Circuit Court of Appeals threw out the case, saying the tobacco companies couldn't sue the EPA over this issue because the report on which the case was based was preliminary and not a final action of the EPA.

The Surgeon General Weighs In

Surgeons generals began looking into the health dangers of secondhand smoke in the 1970s. In 1986, a surgeon general's report linked exposure to ETS with the onset

The Science Regarding Secondhand Smoke
Many government agencies and organizations have
reviewed data regarding the dangers of secondhand
smoke. They include:

• the American Heart Association
• the Centers for Disease Control and Prevention's
  National Institute for Occupational Safety and
  Health
• the National Academy of Sciences
• the U.S. Environmental Protection Agency
• the U.S. Public Health Service

After separate reviews, all these organizations concluded that exposure to secondhand smoke in the
workplace and the home poses increased danger of
cardiovascular disease, lung cancer, stroke, and other
illnesses.

of lung cancer, and in 2006 Surgeon General Richard H.
Carmona's report, *The Health Consequences of Involuntary
Exposure to Tobacco Smoke*, declared, "The debate is over .
. . the scientific evidence is now *indisputable*." According to
the report, secondhand smoke contains more than fifty
cancer-causing chemicals, and exposure to ETS at work
or at home increases a person's risk by 25 to 30 percent
for developing cardiac disease and by 20 to 30 percent
for developing lung cancer. It also concluded that nearly
half of Americans are still exposed to ETS on a regular
basis.

The surgeon general agrees with the National Institutes of Health, the American Cancer Society, and the EPA. All have concluded that children are at particular risk from exposure to secondhand smoke: "Among infants to 18 months of age, secondhand smoke is associated with as many as 300,000 cases of bronchitis and pneumonia each year." Children who are asthmatic also experience additional and more severe asthma attacks because of ETS exposure.

Laws Regarding Secondhand Smoke

Despite what is known about the cancer-causing effects of secondhand smoke, like other federal regulatory agencies, the EPA does not have authority to regulate tobacco or smoking. In an effort to protect nonsmokers from being forced to breathe tobacco smoke and suffer its potentially harmful health consequences, state and local governments have followed the federal government's lead in making public buildings smoke-free.

State and local governments are able to regulate smoking in public places, if they choose to do so. The DOJ has had preliminary success in prosecuting its racketeering case, but it won't have a big effect on regulating the industry. In order for meaningful national regulation to happen, Congress has to pass a law.

CHAPTER 7

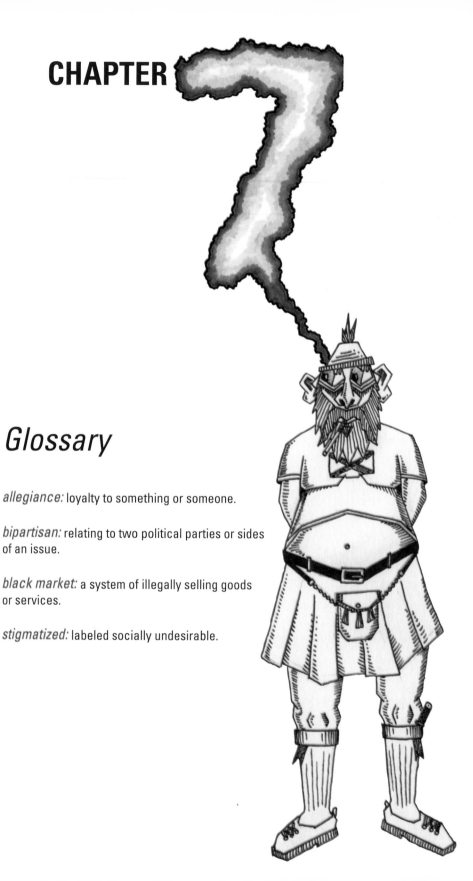

Glossary

allegiance: loyalty to something or someone.

bipartisan: relating to two political parties or sides of an issue.

black market: a system of illegally selling goods or services.

stigmatized: labeled socially undesirable.

Where Do We Go from Here?

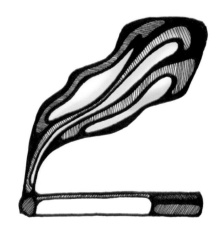

A 2007 survey of 800 American voters showed that the majority (70 percent) support legislation that would give the FDA authority to regulate tobacco. Take a look at some of the poll results:

- 63 percent of smokers and 74 percent of nonsmokers support regulation of tobacco by the FDA.
- 72 percent of Republicans, 71 percent of Democrats, and 68 percent of independents support regulation of tobacco by the FDA.

(*Source*: Poll conducted by Public Opinion Strategies and the Mellman Group)

Could FDA Jurisdiction Lead to a Tobacco Ban?

Historically, the tobacco industry has feared coming under FDA jurisdiction because cigarette manufacturers did not know what kinds of inspections and restrictions the FDA might place on them. Of course, the industry's ultimate fear is that the FDA would pursue an all-out ban on tobacco. However, there are good reasons to believe that will never happen.

For one thing, several southern states have a strong economic link to the industry. Tobacco farmers, everyone employed in the manufacturing of tobacco products, those who transport the products to market, and businesses that sell them to the public would all oppose a ban. Additionally, there is a fear that, should tobacco products be banned, a lucrative *black market* for tobacco products might develop, much like the one that currently exists for illegal drugs.

Though a tobacco ban seems unlikely, poll results indicate that the majority of Americans want the FDA to regulate tobacco. In order to accomplish that, the Supreme Court has already ruled that Congress would need to pass legislation granting that authority to the FDA.

All It Would Take Is a Law

In 1998, after the FDA's Supreme Court defeat, Senators John McCain (R–Arizona) and Kent Conrad (D–North Dakota) introduced legislation to regulate tobacco. When it seemed like the bill would pass, the tobacco industry launched a massive advertising campaign against it, and senators who opposed the bill loaded it with amendments they knew those in favor of the bill

Pulling the Wool over Your Eyes

Watch for tactics like these when industries want to influence Congress or the public. The tobacco industry has used all of them:

- **Focus public attention on other issues:** Advocates for Big Tobacco may flood newspapers with letters to the editor urging people to focus on "more important issues," such as crime or education in our public schools rather than smoking. They will write and email television reporters with the same message.
- **Deflect questions:** Instead of answering questions directly, advocates for tobacco will talk long enough to steer the discussion to another issue, such as the plight of farmers or economic issues, rather than to the health crisis caused by smoking.
- **Flood congressional offices:** Advocates of unrestricted tobacco use make telephone calls and send letters and e-mails to their government representatives, pushing their point of view.
- **Criticize adversaries:** One effective strategy is to talk about how the FDA isn't doing a good job in some other area rather than whether it would be a good idea for the agency to regulate tobacco.
- **Develop "talking points":** For example, tobacco advocates will talk about the Constitution and an adult's right to smoke rather than the dangers of addiction. They will get allies "on the same page," making sure that everyone in the industry knows what the talking points are and using every opportunity to repeat them in public forums.
- **Reframe the debate:** Instead of talking about health, tobacco advocates will consistently remind people how much they hate "prohibitions."
- **File lawsuits:** Pro-tobacco advocates may try to intimidate opponents or scare the masses by suing a few organizations for huge sums. After ABC aired a documentary on smoking in the 1990s, for example, Philip Morris sued the network for $10 billion, alleging that the program made "false and defamatory" statements about the tobacco company.

would oppose. Ultimately, the bill failed. Had it passed, it would have put advertising restrictions on the manufacturers and cost the industry approximately twice as much as the MSA, while offering less protection against future lawsuits. What the law would not have done, however, is put tobacco under FDA jurisdiction.

In 2007, the Senate and the House of Representatives introduced identical bills into the 110th Congress— Senate bill S.625 and House bill H.R.1108. Both had *bipartisan* support. Among other things, the proposed law would:

- provide the FDA with authority to regulate the manufacture, marketing, and distribution of tobacco products.
- authorize the FDA to set national standards controlling the manufacture of tobacco products and the identity, public disclosure, and amount of ingredients used in such products.
- provide new and flexible enforcement authority to ensure that there is effective oversight of the tobacco industry's efforts to develop, introduce, and promote less harmful tobacco products.
- vest the FDA with the authority to regulate the levels of tar, nicotine, and other harmful components in tobacco products.
- require tobacco product manufacturers to disclose previously unavailable research, as well as findings generated in the future.

If passed, this law would not make tobacco illegal, and it would not remove any controls currently exercised by the Department of Agriculture. More than 500 public health organizations, faith-based groups, and other organizations support the bill. With support like this, you'd think it would be easy to pass a law. As history proves, it can be very difficult to pass a law in Congress regulating Big Tobacco.

A Look at the Tobacco Lobby

The tobacco industry spends millions of dollars every year to influence members of Congress. Campaign con-

In 2007, the United States Congress passed a bill that would allow the FDA to control the use of tobacco, finally acknowledging that tobacco is a drug.

tributions, travel expenses, expensive fund-raisers, contributions to favorite charities—the list of ways to influence members of Congress is long. When members of Congress accept such gifts or contributions, they often feel they owe *allegiance* to the supportive industry.

Lobbyists can be powerfully persuasive. Many were once members of Congress themselves; others were employees of the government agencies they later lobby Congress about. Their comprehensive understanding of how a particular government agency works or the personal friendships forged while working for the government can make them very effective spokespeople for particular industries.

It's Amazing What Money Can Buy

The influence of tobacco companies extends far beyond Congress. Big Tobacco has a lot of money, and it can afford to employ some of the best lawyers and scientists in the country. Among the lawyers who have worked for the industry are a former Supreme Court law clerk, a Rhodes scholar, and a former chief counsel for the FDA. In fact, many lawyers who once worked for the FDA move on to employment with tobacco companies. The same is true of scientists. The first director of the Council for Tobacco Research (CTR) was a former university president and cancer researcher whose resume included employment with both the American Cancer Society and the National Cancer Institute. Additionally, cigarette companies have given large sums to some of the most prestigious hospitals and professional associations in the country.

In 1982 and 1983, Congress held hearings on labeling of tobacco products. According to Judge Kessler's findings in *United States of America v. Philip Morris USA Inc.*, *et al.*, many of the scientific witnesses who testified at the 1982 and 1983 hearings "were tobacco industry consultants who were receiving funding from the lawyers' Special Account No. 4." The judge's observation that tobacco company money financed these scientists' work raises questions about their testimony. Was it unbiased or did the money they received influence what they had to say?

Despite some setbacks, the tobacco industry remains very powerful. Over the years, it has been able to use

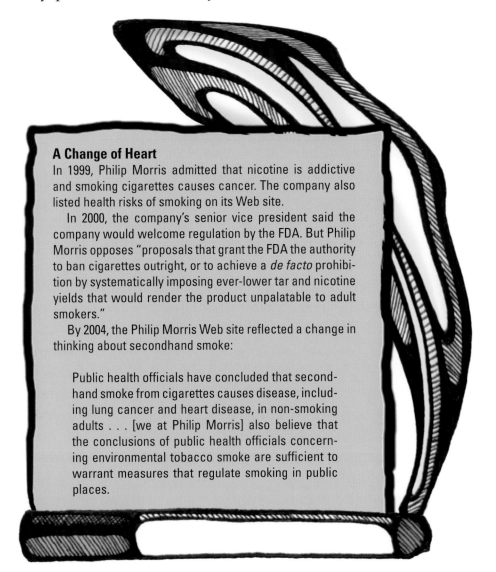

A Change of Heart

In 1999, Philip Morris admitted that nicotine is addictive and smoking cigarettes causes cancer. The company also listed health risks of smoking on its Web site.

In 2000, the company's senior vice president said the company would welcome regulation by the FDA. But Philip Morris opposes "proposals that grant the FDA the authority to ban cigarettes outright, or to achieve a *de facto* prohibition by systematically imposing ever-lower tar and nicotine yields that would render the product unpalatable to adult smokers."

By 2004, the Philip Morris Web site reflected a change in thinking about secondhand smoke:

> Public health officials have concluded that secondhand smoke from cigarettes causes disease, including lung cancer and heart disease, in non-smoking adults . . . [we at Philip Morris] also believe that the conclusions of public health officials concerning environmental tobacco smoke are sufficient to warrant measures that regulate smoking in public places.

its power to influence decisions regarding its own regulation. Yet many laws have passed that do place some controls over the industry. The issue of how far America wants to go in regulating tobacco remains an open question, however.

Cigarette Taxes

The American government has taxed tobacco since 1794, just after the Revolutionary War. In fact, tobacco taxes paid for much of the Revolutionary War, the Civil War, and other wars, right up through the Korean War in the 1950s. Cigarette taxes have also been used to address budget shortfalls over the years. While there is consensus among the public that people should stop smoking, to many it seems as though we have come to depend on the cigarette tax.

Each time an American buys a package of cigarettes, a percentage of the purchase price goes to pay a federal excise tax and another portion goes to pay state taxes. Some of the purchase price may also go to local taxes. All these taxes have been increasing. This, and the payments made to the states through the MSA, would seem to indicate that the government has a stake in the continuing success of the tobacco industry.

Cigarette taxes are often touted as a way of discouraging people from purchasing cigarettes, and that seems like a good idea. But if the goal is to wean everyone off cigarettes, other funding sources must be found for the things currently supported by cigarette taxes.

Some people wonder if it is fair to ask smokers, many of whom are struggling to quit smoking, to pay high taxes on the cigarettes they can't currently resist purchasing. This may be an especially important question when we realize that smoking is increasingly becoming a class issue. When the tobacco industry glamorized smoking before the 1960s, people at every income level indulged in the habit. But as the dangers of smoking have become better known and the habit has become *stigmatized*, it is people with less education (and consequently less income) who are most likely to smoke. Do we want them to be the primary financial supporters of some of our most important government programs?

So Where Do We Stand Today?

At least 15 million Americans have died of smoking-related diseases since 1964, and each year approximately 400,000 fatalities are added to that number. While there is no law banning tobacco, there are countless laws regulating its advertising, availability, and use. Antismoking education has been rigorous and successful, but not successful enough. Clearly, many people are alive today because they made the decision not to smoke that first cigarette, yet 20 percent of adults still smoke.

The majority of Americans seem to believe that while people have a right to smoke, it is sensible not to do so. Those who do smoke usually make that decision before age twenty. If you make it to age twenty without smoking, chances are you will never take up the habit. Surveys consistently show that those who do become smokers eventually regret having done so.

America may never ban tobacco or even increase restrictions on its use beyond where they are today, but as individuals, we each have the power to ban all forms of tobacco in our own lives. When faced with the choice to use tobacco, opt instead for a long life. Don't smoke.

Further Reading

Brandt, Allan M. *The Cigarette Century: The Rise, Fall, and Deadly Persistence of the Product that Defined America.* New York: Basic Books, 2007.

Esherick, Joan. *Clearing the Haze: A Teen's Guide to Smoking-Related Health Issues.* Philadelphia: Mason Crest, 2005.

Gately, Iain. *Tobacco: A Cultural History of How an Exotic Plant Seduced Civilization.* New York: Grove Press, 2001.

Goodman, Jordan (ed.). *Tobacco in History and Culture: An Encyclopedia.* Farmington Hills, Mich.: Thomson Gale, 2005.

Heyes, Eileen. *Tobacco U.S.A.: The Industry Behind the Smoke Curtain.* Minneapolis: Twenty-First Century Books, 1999.

Hyde, Margaret O., and John F. Setaro. *Smoking 101: An Overview for Teens.* Minneapolis: Twenty-First Century Books, 2005.

Stewart, Gail B. *Understanding Issues: Smoking.* San Diego: KidHaven Press, 2002.

For More Information

Campaign for Tobacco-free Kids
www.tobaccofreekids.org

Chronology of FDA Rule
tobaccofreekids.org/reports/fda/chronology.shtml

Kids' Health: Smoking Stinks
www.kidshealth.org/kid/watch/house/smoking.html

National Institutes of Health, National Cancer Institute:
Smoking: Facts and Tips for Quitting
dccps.nci.nih.gov/TCRB/Smoking_Facts/facts.html

Surgeon General's Warning
www.gdcada.org/statistics/tobacco/surgeon/general.
htm

Teen Antismoking Resources
www.notobacco.org

The Tobacco Timeline
www.tobacco.org/History/Tobacco_History.html

Tobacco Under Attack—A Brief History of Tobacco
www.cnn.com/US/9705/tobacco/history/index.html

World Health Organization: The Top 10 Causes of Death
www.who.int/mediacentre/factsheets/fs310/en/
index2.html

Bibliography

Alcohol and Tobacco Tax and Trade Bureau, U.S. Department of the Treasury. http://www.ttb.gov/about/history.shtml.

Americans for Nonsmoker's Rights. "Secondhand Smoke: Tobacco Industry Attacks." August 2004. http://www.no-smoke.org/document.php?id=278.

Borio, Gene. "Tobacco Timeline: The Twentieth Century 1900–1949—The Rise of the Cigarette." Tobacco.org, Tobacco News and Information. http://www.tobacco.org/resources/history/Tobacco_History20-1.html

Cummings, K. Michael. "Programs and policies to discourage the use of tobacco products." Oncogene 21 (October 2002): 10–17.

Derthick, Martha A. *Up in Smoke: From Legislation to Litigation in Tobacco Politics*. Washington, D.C.: CQ Press, 2002.

Federal Communications Commission. http://www.fcc.gov.

Glantz, Stanton A., John Slade, Lisa A. Bero, Peter Hanauer, and Deborah E. Barnes. *The Cigarette Papers*. Berkeley: University of California Press, 1996.

Kessler, David. *A Question of Intent: A Great American Battle with a Deadly Industry*. New York: Public Affairs, 2001.

"Man Wins $1.1 Million from Big Tobacco." injuryboard.com.http://www.injuryboard.com/view. cfm/Article=578.

Master Settlement Agreement. Office of the Attorney General, State of California, Department of Justice. http://ag.ca.gov/tobacco/msa.php.

Rabin, Robert L., and Stephen D. Sugarman. *Regulating Tobacco*. New York: Oxford University Press, 2001.

Snell, William M., "The U.S. Tobacco Program: How It Works and Who Pays for It." http://www.ca.uky.edu/ age/pubs/aec/aec82/aec82.htm.

State of Connecticut Attorney General's Office. "Connecticut Lawsuit Against the Tobacco Companies." http://www.ct.gov/ag/cwp/view. asp?A=1771&Q=291124.

Surgeon General, Secondhand Smoke. http://www. surgeongeneral.gov/library/secondhandsmoke/ report/index.pdf.

United States Department of Health and Human Services, Centers for Disease Control and Prevention. "Federal Policy and Legislation." http://www. cdc.gov/tobacco/data_statistics/by_topic/policy/ legislation.htm.

United States Department of Health and Human Services, Office of the Surgeon General. http://www. surgeongeneral.gov/aboutoffice.html.

United States Department of Health and Human Services, Office of the Surgeon General. "The Health Consequences of Involuntary Exposure to Tobacco Smoke: A Report of the Surgeon General," June 27, 2006. http://www.surgeongeneral.gov/library/secondhandsmoke.

United States Department of Health and Human Services, Office of the Surgeon General. http://www.surgeongeneral.gov/library/reports.htm.

United States Environmental Protection Agency. "EPA Designates Passive Smoking a 'Class A' or Known Human Carcinogen." http://www.epa.gov/history/topics/smoke/01.htm.

United States Food and Drug Administration. "Comments of Vector Tobacco Inc." www.fda.gov/ohms/dockets/dailys/02/Aug02/080502/01/-0571_c000002_01_vol1.pdf-.

United States Food and Drug Administration. Federal Food, Drug, and Cosmetic Act. http://www.fda.gov/opacom/laws/fdcat/fdctoc.htm.

Index

Picture Credits

Centers for Disease Control and Prevention (CDC): p. 90

Dreamstime.com
  Alistaircotton: p. 86
  Iofoto: p. 62
  Mikessssss: p. 15
  Millan: p. 89
  Lisafx: p. 28
  Rapunzel74: p. 90
  Showface: p. 99

istockphoto.com
  Compucow: p. 84
  Stefan Klein, Stefan: p. 38
  Twitty, Francis: p. 55

National Cancer Institute
  Branson, Bill, pp. 25, 45

National Library of Medicine (NLM): pp. 17, 19, 67

Tobaccodocuments.org: p. 60
  Lorillard: p. 79
  RJ Reynolds Tobacco Co.: p. 72, 75

To the best knowledge of the publisher, all other images are in the public domain. If any image has been inadvertently uncredited, please notify Harding House Publishing Service, Vestal, New York 13850, so that rectification can be made for future printings.

Author/Consultant Biographies

Author

Joyce Libal is a writer and editor living in northeastern Pennsylvania. She has written numerous educational books.

Consultant

Wade Berrettini, the consultant for *Smoking: The Dangerous Addiction*, received his MD from Jefferson Medical College and a PhD in Pharmacology from Thomas Jefferson University. For ten years, Dr. Berrettini served as a Fellow at the National Institutes of Health in Bethesda, Maryland, where he studied the genetics of behavioral disorders. Currently Dr. Berrettini is the Karl E. Rickels Professor of Psychiatry and Director, Center for Neurobiology and Behavior at the University of Pennsylvania in Philadelphia. He is also an attending physician at the Hospital of the University of Pennsylvania.

Dr. Berrettini is the author or co-author of more than 250 scientific articles as well as several books. He has conducted ground-breaking genetic research in nicotine addiction. He is the holder of two patents and the recipient of several awards, including recognition by Best Doctors in America 2003–2004, 2005–2006, and 2007–2008.